Dementia Caregiving 101

Practical Strategies to Build a Support System, Navigate Medical & Legal Challenges with Ease, and Improve the Quality of Life for You and Your Loved Ones

Debra Lewis RN, BSN

Table of Contents

Introduction

One minute, you are celebrating family occasions and making plans for new adventures together. You look around at your parents, aunts, uncles, and grandparents and think about how significant they have been in your life and in creating the person you have become today. Maybe you are even sitting around with your children, watching them hang on to every word your loved one says as they spin tales that link the past to future generations. It's comforting.

At first, there is nothing to worry about. It's a little bit of forgetfulness here and there, and you put it down to typical memory loss with age. Before you know it, there is this nagging feeling in your gut that something just isn't right—and then the diagnosis comes. As you hear the word "dementia," time slows down, and you can feel the weight of the world falling on your entire body. No matter how cheerful you try to remain, you can't shake the thought that it's all downhill from here.

Watching a loved one suffer from dementia is excruciating. Watching someone you love and respect go through the initial symptoms of dementia is awful. But not as awful as the day that they don't recognize who you are. At the same time, caring for someone with dementia can be incredibly frustrating. How do you handle someone who is convinced they are on a bus and about to get off at the next stop when they are sitting in their favorite armchair? How can you tell your own parents that they can't drive or have a bank card any longer? On top of that, there is your constant fear for their safety.

When my father was diagnosed with vascular dementia, I was convinced that my thirty-four years as a registered nurse had prepared me for the challenge ahead. But the disease took him from us far too quickly. As my mother's journey through a slower progression of the same illness began, I realized nothing could have fully prepared me for the realities of being a caregiver to my own parents. Each day brought new challenges, unexpected demands, and deep emotional strains—experiences that reshaped my understanding of both dementia and caregiving.

I have spent over three decades in nursing, caring for countless patients across various stages of life and illness. Yet, when it came to providing care for my own parents, I found myself on steep learning curves, facing situations that no textbook had covered. This contrast between my professional knowledge and the practical realities of dementia care is what drives this book. It's created not just from a nurse's perspective but from a daughter's heart—a heart that knows the pain and exhaustion of caring for loved ones with dementia.

Dementia Caregiving 101 is designed to fill the resource gap that caregivers so often encounter. Here, you will find a blend of practical strategies with emotional support to guide you through the complexities of dementia care. This book is your companion, offering step-by-step advice on daily caregiving tasks, advanced care techniques, and much-needed emotional support for you and your loved one.

As we explore these pages together, you will find detailed chapters on managing daily activities, legal advice tailored for dementia care, nutritional strategies, and exercise plans that cater to dementia patients. Emotional well-being is a core theme throughout this book, emphasizing the importance of self-care for caregivers, for you cannot pour from an empty cup.

This book is written for you—from someone who has walked in similar shoes and understands the highs and lows of this journey. It aims to be a source of strength and a testament to the resilience required in dementia caregiving. Here, you'll find actionable solutions, a community understanding, and shared experiences. Together, we will be able to handle the challenges but also find joy in these precious moments with our loved ones. Trust me, you are going to need a good sense of humor throughout this journey, so I promise it's not all doom and gloom.

Engage with this book as your guide and companion. Use it to navigate the tough days and to find meaningful moments in your caregiving role. Reach out to support networks, apply the strategies discussed, and remember, you are not alone. We can foster a caregiving environment that brings dignity, comfort, and quality of life to our loved ones while ensuring our own well-being remains a priority—and without feeling guilty about this. I truly wish that I had reached out and taken advantage of the resources that were available to me when I was caring for my parents.

Let's begin this journey with hope and determination, ready to face the challenges ahead and discover the unexpected joys of caring deeply for someone who once cared for us. Caregiving is not just about survival; it's about finding a way to thrive—for them and you.

Chapter 1

Understanding Dementia and Its Impacts

When my mother first began to forget to pay the bills, it was easy to dismiss her mistakes as mere slips of memory—something we all experience. But my mom was a bookkeeper by trade her entire life. She was a financial guru and could run the family budget with her eyes closed. When she later started sending money to any cause that was advertised on television, the reality of the situation settled in with a weight that was both terrifying and heart-wrenching. When my gentle-giant father began lashing out both verbally and physically at my mom, we were so confused. My dad worshiped my mom. How could he be acting this way?

My parent's behavior was not simply aging; this was dementia. Each experience of caring for my parents taught me something profoundly new about this complex condition, which does not discriminate and changes lives forever. In this chapter, we will explore what dementia entails, from its various types to the symptoms that may signal its onset and the critical importance of an accurate diagnosis.

Decoding Dementia: Types, Symptoms, and Diagnosis

Dementia is an umbrella term for a range of neurological conditions with varying symptoms that severely affect memory, thinking skills, and social abilities and interfere with daily functioning. For some sufferers, feelings and behavior can be affected, which can then influence their relationships (Alzheimer's Association-d, n.d.). Dementia is not a single disease but a general term that covers a broad spectrum of specific medical conditions, including Alzheimer's disease and vascular dementia.

Alzheimer's disease is the most common type of dementia, accounting for an estimated 60 to 80 percent of cases. In Alzheimer's, two types of proteins accumulate in the brain: plaques (beta-amyloid) and tangles (tau). These proteins disrupt communications between nerve cells and lead to cell death. Symptoms often start gradually and worsen over time, affecting memory, language, and other cognitive abilities (World Health Organization, 2023).

Vascular dementia, which is the disease that affected my father, is the second most common type of dementia. It arises from other conditions that block or reduce blood flow to the brain, depriving the brain cells of oxygen and nutrients. Individuals with this form of dementia may experience markedly abrupt changes in their speed of thinking, problem-solving, concentration, and organization, although memory loss can also be an issue. A stroke, multiple small strokes, or damage to blood vessels may be the cause of vascular dementia. Sadly,

Alzheimer's and vascular dementia often present together (Mayo Clinic, 2021).

Lewy body dementia occurs from abnormal protein build-up inside nerve cells, called Lewy bodies. This type of dementia can affect the brain as well as other bodily functions, such as vision, movement, and mood. This type of dementia shares characteristics with both Alzheimer's disease and Parkinson's disease, with common symptoms including memory loss, attention deficits, and physical coordination issues. Lewy body dementia is another progressive disease that gets worse with time. Symptoms can appear after the age of fifty (NIH, n.d.), unlike Alzheimer's, which tends to manifest after the age of sixty.

Frontotemporal dementia (FTD), on the other hand, tends to affect younger adults compared to other forms of dementia. It involves the degeneration of nerve cells in the frontal and temporal lobes of the brain until the lobes begin to shrink. There are two main types of FTD. The frontal variant type affects behavior and personality, whereas the primary progressive aphasia type can be classified as either progressive nonfluent aphasia or semantic dementia. Progressive nonfluent aphasia affects speech, and semantic dementia impacts the way a person uses and understands language. This means symptoms can vary from socially inappropriate behaviors to a lack of empathy to physical symptoms, like tremors and poor coordination (Johns Hopkins Medicine, 2024.)

I know those were a lot of huge words, and it is difficult to understand if you are not in the medical profession. However, recognizing the symptoms of dementia early on is fundamental for managing the disease effectively. Common early symptoms across most types of dementia include:

- Memory loss, especially of recent events
- Difficulties with problem-solving or planning
- Struggles with everyday tasks
- Reduced concentration
- Behavioral changes
- Confusion over time or location
- Challenges in understanding visual images and spatial relationships.
- Changes in mood or personality, such as increased irritability, anxiety, or depression (Better Health, n.d.)

For example, when my mother got lost on her way home, it showed us that her sense of direction was getting worse. We later found ways to manage this better through the proper support and changes at home. Because dementia has such a vast array of symptoms, it's essential to watch out for individual changes in your loved ones. My mother got lost on a journey that she knew like the back of her hand, but you might notice your loved one not being able to make other decisions, like what to wear on a cold day—something that they wouldn't have had problems with previously.

Navigating the dementia diagnosis process involves various assessments, including medical history evaluation, physical examinations, laboratory tests, neurological tests, mental status tests, and brain imaging. There may also be psychiatric assessments because of the comorbidity with anxiety and depression (Better Health, n.d.). Early and accurate diagnosis can significantly affect the management of the condition, allowing for timely intervention and planning. I know this can be challenging, especially if your loved one denies there is anything wrong. If this is the case, you can still contact your doctor or local community health center for more advice.

Misdiagnosis is a common challenge, as symptoms of dementia can overlap with other conditions like depression or the side effects of medication. This is another reason why getting an early diagnosis is crucial: if you are concerned, you are in a better position to get a second opinion. This can lead to adjustments in treatment plans that better suit the specific needs of the individual.

Understanding these different aspects of dementia can help us better manage the condition, which will no doubt benefit your loved one. It also prepares you as a caregiver to adapt your approach and expectations as the disease progresses. This knowledge empowers you to provide compassionate, informed care that can significantly enhance the quality of life for both you and your loved one.

Progression Patterns: Recognizing Each Stage of Dementia

Understanding how dementia progresses is critical to providing effective care. Dementia typically moves through three stages—early, middle, and late—each bringing its own challenges and needs. Grasping these stages helps anticipate changes and prepare emotionally and practically for what lies ahead. Before we discover more about these stages, please bear in mind that progression will depend on different factors, such as the type of dementia, their age, their physical health and mental health, their lifestyle, and how soon they received a diagnosis after first experiencing symptoms.

In the early stage of dementia, symptoms can be subtle and are often mistaken for typical signs of aging or stress. For instance, memory lapses are common, such as forgetting recent conversations or misplacing items. They could be aware of these signs, but it might be that someone else notices them first. If they are aware of these changes, you might notice their increased anxiety, or they might fear going about their daily tasks. At this stage, individuals may maintain their independence but require reminders for daily tasks.

It's crucial here to foster a supportive environment that allows the individual to function as independently as possible, which can help maintain their self-esteem and slow the progression of cognitive decline. Caregivers should focus on establishing a routine that includes cognitive exercises, social interaction, and physical activity, all tailored to the individual's current abilities.

The care requirements intensify as the disease progresses to the middle stage, often the most prolonged phase. Here, memory issues become more pronounced, with individuals possibly forgetting their personal history or failing to recognize their close family members' faces. I have always said that "fascinating" is the wrong word to use, but at this stage, you might find yourself wondering what exactly goes through their minds. You may hear your loved one talking about "going home" when they are already home because they are thinking about childhood homes or witness them talking about their own parents as if they are still alive.

Communication becomes more of a challenge as the individual might need help finding words or following along with conversations. You may need to work on your patience as your loved ones begin to repeat the same questions only minutes after asking them. During this stage, safety becomes a primary concern, particularly if they are waking up in the middle of the night. Simple home modifications can make a huge difference, such as removing rugs to prevent falls or installing grab bars in the bathroom. Caregivers need to be more involved in daily activities, providing more direct assistance with personal care and supervision to ensure safety, more so if you find them wobbly on their feet.

Communicating effectively in the middle stage requires patience and understanding. Strategies such as using simple, straightforward language and speaking calmly and reassuringly can help. Nonverbal cues like gestures and facial expressions to aid comprehension and convey empathy are also helpful. Keeping instructions straightforward and breaking tasks into manageable steps can reduce frustration for the caregiver and the individual with dementia. Please refrain from any phrases that start with "Remember..." This is a hard habit to break, but you aren't doing yourself any favors, and you may end up upsetting them.

Near-total dependence and significant physical decline mark the late stage of dementia. Communication at this point may be limited to non-verbal cues, but understanding these subtle signs becomes vital. As the disease progresses, loved ones can become more and more disorientated. The concept of time fades, and they seem to spend more time living in the past. Challenging their understanding may cause them to become distressed. Perspective can really help you at this point. Imagine looking at yourself in the mirror and expecting to see the fifteen-year-old version of yourself. The fifteen-year-old version of yourself doesn't have children, so it can cause great confusion when you talk to them about their children or grandchildren and assume they will remember their faces (Dementia UK, 2023).

Caregivers might find themselves doing most, if not all, of the daily care tasks as the individual's mobility significantly decreases, which can be physically and emotionally draining. Your loved ones may have difficulties eating and drinking, so it becomes harder for them to get the right nutrients and stay hydrated. Some people won't remember that they have eaten and feel the need to eat more. Others may not recognize when they are hungry or have trouble communicating their hunger (Livewell, 2021).

It's crucial during this stage to seek additional help, whether from family members, professional caregivers, or community resources. This stage is also the time to consider more comprehensive medical care options, including hospice or palliative care, which can provide comfort and support in managing end-of-life symptoms.

Planning for future needs throughout these stages is essential. Early on, discussing future care preferences with your loved one can help you make informed decisions later. Legal and financial planning is also crucial early in the diagnosis to ensure that the person's wishes are honored and the family is protected—but don't worry, we will cover this soon. As the disease progresses, these plans may need revisiting and adjusting according to the changing circumstances. Preparing for potential living arrangements, whether that involves home modifications to support aging in place or researching assisted living facilities, should be done proactively, calmly, and thoughtfully.

Behavioral Changes and How to Interpret Them

When my mom called me in the middle of the night because my dad was screaming at her and pushing her, it was one of the most frightening experiences I had ever faced. Initially, I couldn't understand why this sweet and gentle man, who had always been so calm and collected, was suddenly attacking my mom. I learned that such behavioral changes are not uncommon in dementia and that they can manifest in various forms, including aggression, wandering, and sleep disturbances. These behaviors can be deeply distressing for those experiencing them and us as caregivers. Understanding what may trigger these behaviors and how to respond can significantly affect our ability to manage these situations effectively and compassionately.

Aggression in dementia can often be a form of communication. As verbal skills decline, frustration can increase, leading to aggressive behavior. You wouldn't be alone in feeling like your elderly adult seems to have resorted back to child-like behaviors. Known as "age regression," the lack of communication skills or sense of control can cause adults to revert to angry outbursts—think of a toddler who doesn't get their way (Stellar Care, n.d.). When I was talking to a friend at a support group, she told me that her eighty-four-year-old gran with Alzheimer's and vascular dementia had started attempting to bite the care home staff because she didn't want to take her medicine. She also noticed that this behavior only got worse when her mom was around because her mom tended to treat her gran as if she were a child. Physical discomfort, environmental factors, or misunderstood social interactions can trigger this behavior, too.

Wandering, another typical behavior, may occur due to disorientation or a misplaced need to fulfill a forgotten task. Sleep disturbances, including insomnia or increased sleepiness, can be influenced by changes in the brain associated with dementia but also by a lack of daytime activity or psychological factors such as depression.

Managing these behaviors safely and effectively requires a calm, structured approach. Identifying and addressing the underlying cause of aggression is essential—pain, fear, or frustration. Maintaining a predictable routine can help, as can creating a calm environment. It's also vital to ensure personal safety and consider professional advice if the behavior escalates. For wandering, securing the home environment is critical. Using devices, such as door alarms that alert you if your loved one attempts to leave, can prevent both wandering and potential injuries.

As for sleep disturbances, establishing a soothing nighttime routine can be beneficial. Limiting caffeine intake during the day, ensuring adequate physical activity, and using comforting nightlights or relaxing music can help promote better sleep. If nighttime waking and leaving the bed becomes a regular issue, you may want to consider investing in a bed sensor floor mat that sends a signal to a carer once the person stands on it.

Changing the environment can significantly reduce these upsetting behaviors. Reducing noise levels, maintaining a comfortable room temperature, and optimizing lighting to reduce shadows or glare can help reduce anxiety and confusion, which often trigger problematic behaviors. Keep personal items that evoke a sense of calm and familiarity within easy reach and organize spaces to minimize frustration and confusion. For example, labeling cabinets and drawers with both words and visual cues can help individuals find items quickly, reducing feelings of frustration.

Sometimes, the support of neurologists, psychiatrists, or behavioral specialists becomes indispensable. These experts can offer strategies tailored to your loved one's needs, including medication to manage their symptoms more effectively or therapies designed to improve their quality of life. Their guidance can also be invaluable in helping you understand and interpret the under-lying causes of challenging behaviors, ensuring that you are responding in the most effective way possible.

Aside from your patience and understanding, you may find you have to be willing to adapt your approach as the condition evolves. Caring for someone with dementia is a continuous learning process that brings new challenges and insights daily. We sometimes forget (the irony!) that it is the disease and not our loved one making these choices. I know I lost my cool many times with my parents, and I felt terrible afterward. The frustration and fatigue we experience from trying to help them can be over-whelming. By focusing on compassionate, informed care, you can help manage these behaviors in a way that respects your loved one's dignity and enhances their well-being.

Cognitive Decline: Practical Tips for Daily Management

When caring for a loved one with dementia, maintaining a struc-tured daily routine can be a lifeline. This structure doesn't just help to keep things predictable for those with cognitive impair-ments; it also reduces the stress that can trigger confusion or agitation. Establishing a regular schedule of activities catering to the individual's abilities provides a framework that supports cognitive function and emotional well-being. For instance, my father found great comfort in the routine of simple morning walks followed by breakfast at the same time each day. This routine kept him physically active and helped anchor his sense of time and place, often eroded by dementia.

Routine helps cognitive health by strengthening neural pathways through repeated activities, which can help slow mental decline progression. This is called neuroplasticity and explains how the brain can change. Inside the brain, there are billions of neurons that have multiple connections to other neurons. The more often something is repeated, whether a thought or an action, the stronger the neural connection between the neurons grows and the easier it is to retrieve the information (The Ness Care Group, n.d.). If the thought or action isn't repeated, the connections gradually die away.

This was something I found quite fascinating, not just for routines but also for cognitive stimulation. Pop a person with dementia in front of the television for hours on end, and there is little to no need for neurons to make new connections or strengthen existing ones. On the other hand, if you encourage activities like games and coloring, you are giving your loved one brain stimulation and helping neural connections form.

Integrating activities like sorting mail, folding laundry, or setting the table can provide purposeful daily tasks involving problem-solving and fine motor skills. These activities should be adjusted to match the individual's current capabilities, ensuring they are neither too challenging nor overly simplistic, which can lead to frustration or disinterest. For example, if someone is used to enjoying complex puzzles but now struggles with them, switching to more straightforward jigsaw puzzles can provide a sense of accomplishment without the stress of failure. Incorporating cognitive stimulation into everyday activities is essential and beneficial.

Simple memory games, like matching pairs or recalling lists, can be enjoyable and beneficial. My parents would play cards for hours some days. Incorporating reading into the daily routine, whether it's the caregiver reading aloud or the person with dementia reading themselves, stimulates language and cognitive skills. The key is to choose materials that are engaging and appropriate for their reading level, which may change as the disease progresses. Even listening to audiobooks can be valuable, providing cognitive stimulation through listening and comprehension.

Technology today offers additional tools to support cognitive function. Devices and apps designed to aid memory, such as reminder applications on tablets or smartphones, can help manage daily tasks and appointments. For those who wander, GPS devices can be a safeguarding tool that brings peace of mind to caregivers while preserving the dignity of their loved ones. Furthermore, automated home systems that control lighting, temperature, and security can reduce the burden on those with dementia by maintaining a stable and safe environment, minimizing the confusion from multiple remote controls or complicated interfaces. Many of these devices are very inexpensive and easy to find on places like Amazon.

Adapting these tools and activities to fit within a well-structured daily routine is more of an art than a science, requiring ongoing adjustment and patience. As abilities change, so must the activities and tools we employ to ensure they remain appropriate and supportive of cognitive health. This adaptive approach maximizes the quality of life for those with dementia while supporting caregivers by providing a clear framework for daily care activities.

Emotional Repercussions for Patients and How to Handle Them

One of the most heart-wrenching aspects of dementia is witnessing the emotional turmoil it can bring to your loved one.

Imagine the distress when someone dear does not recall significant life events or familiar faces. This confusion often manifests as anxiety, depression, or withdrawal from social interactions—signs that are painful to observe and can be equally challenging to manage. Recognizing these signs of emotional distress is crucial in providing the support your loved one needs.

Anxiety might appear as restlessness or sudden difficulty in settling down. At the same time, depression in dementia might not always be apparent, manifesting as apathy or a lack of interest in previously enjoyed activities. Withdrawal from social interactions is particularly noticeable when individuals who were once vibrant and outgoing seem to shrink from conversations or avoid gatherings they once looked forward to.

Addressing these emotional upheavals starts with acknowledging and validating your loved one's feelings. Active listening plays a vital role here; it involves more than hearing words—it's about understanding the emotions behind them. Active listening means giving your loved ones the opportunity to finish their sentences without interrupting them or getting frustrated when it takes them longer to express themselves than it used to. The same can be said for answering questions. One of my biggest regrets in my role as my parent's caregiver is that I was always so busy trying to get everything done that many times I didn't just sit down and talk to them, to listen to them and ignore any distractions that, in hindsight, weren't important. When your loved one expresses confusion or distress, acknowledge their feelings without reinforcing their fears. Phrases like, "It seems like you're feeling lost. It's okay to feel that way. I'm right here with you" can provide immense comfort. Remember, validating isn't about agreeing that their misconceived worries are valid, but affirming their feelings is essential.

Another way to reduce emotional distress is to adapt the way you communicate with them. You may need to speak more slowly and shorten the length of your sentences. Watch your tone for any hints of impatience, and the same can be said for your body language. Sharp movements with your hands and arms can be a sign of irritation, and this could agitate your loved one. Make eye contact as you are talking to them so that they can see you are giving them your full attention. No matter what happens, try not to patronize them or speak to them as if they are children. Keep to the same physical level as they are at so as not to tower over them and intimidate them (NIDirect, n.d.).

Maintaining social interactions is crucial. Social activities stimulate emotional and cognitive functions and can boost mood significantly. Facilitating these interactions might involve helping your loved one connect with friends and family through scheduled visits or video calls. My parent's favorite thing to do was FaceTime all their grandchildren. They could be having the worst day, and one of the kids would FaceTime them, and it was like their frustrations just washed away.

For those more advanced in their dementia progression, group activities in a controlled, familiar environment—such as sing-alongs or simple group exercises—can encourage participation and interaction in a non-threatening way. My mom loved to be involved in many social activities, but my dad preferred to be alone. It's important to tailor social activities to the individual's current capabilities and comfort levels, ensuring that these don't become sources of stress.

Behavioral redirection techniques are also invaluable. When you notice a person becomes triggered by a certain situation and intense emotions appear or their dementia symptoms worsen, redirect their attention to a different activity (Hipp, 2024). For instance, if a puzzle annoys a person, put it away. Suggesting a walk outside or looking through a family photo album might shift their focus to happier stimuli.

Dealing with the emotional aspects of dementia is as crucial as managing the physical symptoms—perhaps even more so, as emotional health directly impacts physical well-being (WebMD, 2023). Each step to understand, engage, and soothe your loved one helps manage the disease and strengthens your connection with them, providing moments of joy and peace amidst the challenges. This deep, empathetic approach to caregiving ensures that you can foster an environment where your loved one feels valued and understood despite the hardships.

The Science of Dementia: What Caregivers Need to Know About Neurology

Understanding the brain's role in dementia can be as complex as the condition. Yet, grasping these basics can reveal a lot about what your loved one is experiencing. For instance, one of the hallmarks of Alzheimer's disease is the buildup of amyloid plaques. These sticky accumulations gather outside nerve cells and comprise a protein fragment called beta-amyloid. This buildup is critical to understand because these plaques block cell-to-cell signaling at synapses and are believed to contribute to cell death. Alzheimer's also damages connections between neurons, starting with those connections that are associated with memories (NIH, 2024).

Neurofibrillary tangles are another culprit, mostly found inside the brain's cells and made mainly of a protein called tau, hence the other name—tau tangles. In a healthy brain, tau helps transport nutrients throughout cells, but there have to be a particular structure for this to happen. However, in Alzheimer's, tau proteins change shape and assemble themselves into tangled structures that disrupt cell transport systems. This disruption leads to the malnourishment of cells, which eventually die (Findley, 2024). These changes explain much of the cognitive decline seen in Alzheimer's patients, such as memory loss and confusion, as these damaged cells are critical to the processing and storage of information. This can be exasperated when combined with vascular dementia because the reduced blood flow to the brain also kills cells (Alzheimer's Association, n.d.-c.).

The impact of these neurological changes on behavior is significant and can be confusing to witness. For example, the death of cells in particular areas of the brain can lead to the loss of specific functions, depending on the region affected. Damage in the frontal lobe, often seen in frontotemporal dementia, can lead to changes in personality and social behavior, making someone once reserved act out of character, perhaps becoming uninhibited or socially inappropriate. The frontal lobe is responsible for emotional expression, language, problem-solving, judgment, sexual behavior, and memory (Healthline, 2023). Understanding these connections between brain changes and behavior can help caregivers better empathize with their loved ones and respond more effectively to their needs.

Recent research in neurology continues to shed light on these processes and offers hope for new treatments. Advances in imaging technologies, for example, now allow researchers to see the buildup of amyloid plaques and tau tangles in living brains rather than waiting until after a patient's death to confirm a diagnosis (Findley, 2024). These advances aid in early detection, monitoring the progression of the disease, and the effectiveness of treatments. There are also exciting developments in potential therapies that target these proteins directly, aiming to slow their accumulation or even remove them from the brain (Gregory 2023).

Applying these neurological insights to caregiving can improve caregiving practices. One practical way to help is by changing the living environment to support cognitive function and compensate for lost abilities. For example, knowing that someone with hippocampus damage may have trouble with spatial orientation can lead to reorganizing living spaces to be easier to navigate and more intuitive. Clear labeling of rooms and cupboards, consistent furniture placement, and avoiding clutter are simple yet effective strategies that can reduce confusion and prevent accidents.

Also, neurological insights show how important it is to keep up mental and physical activities to help slow cognitive decline. Activities that challenge the brain, such as puzzles and memory games, are not just ways to pass the time; they are vital exercises in stimulating brain function and maintaining neural connections. Physical exercise also plays a critical role in overall health and increasing blood flow to the brain, which can help nourish remaining healthy cells.

Understanding dementia from a neurological perspective does not require a medical degree; it just takes a willingness to learn and apply this knowledge compassionately. Doing so can make a meaningful difference in the effectiveness of your caregiving and the quality of life for your loved one. As we continue to unravel the complexities of the brain, each piece of knowledge gained is a step toward more personalized, effective care strategies, providing hope for the future and practical help in the present.

One would think that being a nurse would have given me an advantage in recognizing and understanding what was happening with my parents. Not so, and not even after experience with dementia patients. Your perspective is skewed when you are so close and in the middle of it. Looking back, I feel such guilt, wishing I had gotten my parents' help sooner. I wonder if it would have helped or changed the outcome. Sadly, there is nothing I can do about this now, but you probably can. Listen to your gut if you feel or know something is "just different" about your loved one. Early diagnosis is beyond essential, and educating yourself on everything about the disease can be so helpful and empowering.

Though this chapter was dedicated to understanding dementia and the science behind it, there were some strategies to help with caring for your loved ones. Needless to say, this wasn't detailed enough. In the next chapter, we will take caregiving to the next level.

Chapter 2

Practical Caregiving Strategies

When I first began caring for my parents, I quickly realized that the rhythm and predictability we often take for granted had vanished from their lives. Each day could be vastly different from the next and filled with uncertainty and confusion. This is where the power of a well-structured daily routine comes into play, not just for simplicity but as a fundamental part of care that anchors both the caregiver and the loved one to a predictable and safe reality. Establishing a daily routine isn't just about organizing tasks; it's about creating an environment where your loved one can thrive despite the challenges posed by dementia.

Establishing a Daily Care Routine: A Step-by-Step Guide

The importance of a structured daily routine in dementia care cannot be overstated. I have four children, and the last two are coming as twins. I had to have a routine to survive. Throw caring for my parents into the mix, and you have a recipe for a complete breakdown on my part!

For someone living with dementia, the world can become a confusing and unpredictable place, so a routine can significantly reduce anxiety and confusion. It's like setting the stage each day with familiar cues and sequences that can help orient your loved ones first thing in the morning and throughout the day. In my experience, something as simple as maintaining regular meal-times and a consistent bedtime can make a profound difference in managing mood swings and improving overall well-being. My mom would sit at the dining room table every day at 5:30 pm, waiting for dinner. Even if dinner wasn't quite ready, she knew it was coming and was happy to sit there.

The routine should start from the moment they wake up. For example, the morning could start by turning the radio on to a specific radio station. When dementia progresses, you may want to change this to a specific song. This can be followed by a series of steps such as washing, dressing, and having breakfast, which helps maintain personal hygiene and instills a sense of normalcy and independence. Each step should be approached with patience, allowing your loved one the time they need to process and participate to the best of their ability.

Balancing activity with rest throughout the day is crucial in dementia care. Overstimulation can be just as problematic as insufficient stimulation. It's about finding that sweet spot where your loved one can engage in activities without feeling over-whelmed. For instance, scheduling more engaging activities in the morning when my father was more alert and energetic and reserving quieter, more relaxing activities for the afternoon worked best for him. Attempting the same routine for my mom wasn't as successful, so things needed to be adapted to suit both of them.

A typical day might include a morning walk followed by a light breakfast. Post-breakfast, engaging in a cognitive activity like a puzzle or some light gardening can be refreshing. However, it's important to watch for signs of fatigue and offer plenty of opportunities for rest. After lunch, a quiet time with soothing music or a favorite movie can provide a much-needed break, both for the caregiver and the loved one.

Integrating essential daily activities like medication intake, meals, and hygiene into the routine should be handled with dignity and respect. For medication, using a pill organizer can help ensure that your loved one takes the right medication at the right time and can turn a potentially confusing process into a straightforward part of the day. Meals should be a time of connection, not stress. Simple, nutritious meals that are easy to eat can make a big difference in how much your loved one enjoys eating and maintains their strength. We will discuss nutrition in detail.

Hygiene is another area where routine plays a critical role. Establishing a regular schedule for bathing, brushing teeth, and other personal care tasks can help make these essential activities part of the daily rhythm. It's important to approach these sensitive activities with empathy, ensuring you respect their comfort and privacy as much as possible. To reduce confusion, it's a good idea to use the habit stacking technique if you need to add new activities. Habit stacking involves introducing a new activity after an already established activity. As the first activity is already part of their routine, it's easier for the second activity to be integrated into part of their day (Clear, n.d.). This is especially true for medication. If your loved one needs to start taking medication, it's good to get into the habit of doing this straight after cleaning their teeth, for example.

While structure is important, so too is flexibility. The abilities and moods of someone with dementia can fluctuate from day to day and even from one hour to the next. Being flexible in the routine can lead to satisfaction on both sides. It's crucial to remain alert to their cues and be ready to adjust the schedule as needed. If your loved one seems particularly tired one morning, it might be a good idea to postpone a more active task to later or even the next day. Even though you know cognitive stimulation or exercise is good for them, attempting to force them will only upset or agitate them, which is unfair to both them and you.

This flexibility also extends to how tasks are performed. For instance, if dressing becomes a struggle, consider clothing that is easier to manage, like pants with elastic waistbands or shirts with magnetic buttons. These minor adjustments can help maintain their ability to participate in their care, which is important for their self-esteem and overall well-being.

The rewards of a routine are immeasurable—a sense of security, improved well-being, and moments of joy and connection are just a few. As caregivers, our goal is not just to manage the day but to enrich it, making each moment as fulfilling and comfortable as possible for our loved ones.

Communication Techniques That Work with Dementia Patients

Communicating effectively with a loved one who has dementia is a crucial part of caregiving, one that changes as the disease progresses. When my mother's ability to express her thoughts began to wane, it became clear that how we spoke to each other needed to change—not just what we said, but how we said it. Simplifying language doesn't mean using baby talk because that's just insulting. It's about making your words more accessible. Using short, clear sentences can drastically improve understanding. For instance, instead of asking, "What would you like to wear today?" you might say, "Would you like to wear your blue shirt or your red sweater?" This makes it easier for your loved one to grasp what you're saying and offers them a simple choice that maintains their dignity.

Asking direct questions is very useful in this communication toolkit. They help by reducing the mental effort needed for processing and responding. Questions that can be answered with a simple "yes" or "no" are often more manageable and less frustrating for someone struggling with cognitive impairment. It's about simplifying things while still showing respect in your interactions. Remember, the goal is to enhance understanding without causing overwhelm, ensuring that your loved one feels engaged and respected in the conversation.

Non-verbal communication cues can often speak louder than words. I noticed that, at first, when my parents' conversations started to dwindle, I started to feel like it was the end of our communication. I would struggle to find topics that would engage them, and this is when that sense of "the lights are on, but nobody's home" came across me. All I could imagine was that this was the end of any connections we had—because I was focusing on words alone.

A warm smile, gentle touch, or a reassuring tone of voice can convey more safety and affection than words might manage. These cues can be particularly powerful in comforting or calming your loved one when they feel agitated or confused. Observing their body language closely can give clues about how they're feeling or what they might need. For example, if they shrink away when approached, they might feel overwhelmed or scared. In such cases, a calm, soft tone and open body language can help reassure them that they're in a safe space.

As mentioned before, active listening gives you the chance to understand more about your loved one's emotions, but as communication skills decline, you may find it easier to read emotional cues through body language. That's not to say active listening is a skill you no longer need.

This might mean paying attention to not just what is said but how it's said—the tone, the pace, and the pauses. For example, if your loved one starts talking in a higher pitch, could this be a sign that they are angry? When verbal responses do come, they may be fragmented or difficult to interpret, but trying to pick up on the key points and emotions can help create a response that addresses the heart of what they're trying to communicate, and this is going to require your full attention.

Avoiding communication breakdowns is crucial, as these can lead to frustration and distress. Common barriers include distractions, environmental noise, and the individual's own frustration or fatigue. Minimizing background noise and distractions during conversations is important. Turning off the TV or moving to a quieter part of the house can help reduce sensory overload, which can be particularly disorienting for someone with dementia. It's also vital to recognize the signs of fatigue in yourself and your loved one and know when to take a break. Trying to push through tiredness or frustration can lead to misunderstandings and may even escalate to distress. Instead, recognizing when it's time to pause and perhaps resume the conversation later can be a more effective strategy. This doesn't mean you are giving up. It's just a chance to step away, regather yourself, and come back to the situation with a new perspective. Perhaps it just takes a couple of minutes to remind yourself it's not your loved one talking; it's the disease!

The complexities of communication as dementia progresses require patience, adaptability, and a deep reservoir of empathy. By focusing on clear, compassionate communication techniques, you can maintain a meaningful connection with your loved ones, ensuring that they feel supported and understood, no matter where they are in their dementia journey.

Managing Sundowning: Strategies for Late-Day Confusion

Sundowning can be one of the more confusing aspects of dementia care, marked by an increase in confusion, anxiety, and agitation as the evening approaches. However, don't let the name make you think it's limited to this time of the day (Alzheimer's Society 2021). Understanding what triggers sundowning and learning how to manage it can make these heightened moments of confusion much smoother and more comfortable for both of you.

Firstly, recognizing what triggers sundowning in your loved one is essential. Common triggers include fatigue, which accumulates throughout the day, low lighting that may cause shadows and visual difficulties, and an internal confusion between day and night that disrupts the body's normal sleep-wake cycle. The same can be said if your loved one doesn't receive enough daylight, as this can impact their internal body clock. Their sundowning might be because they are hungry or in pain, or it could be related to mood disorders or medications they are on. The truth is, the cause of sundowning isn't well understood yet, so it's important to pay attention to what triggers your loved one (Alzheimer's Society 2021). By paying close attention to these triggers, you can anticipate and mitigate the factors that worsen late-day confusion. For example, you might notice that on days filled with lots of activity, the confusion in the evening is markedly worse. This observation can guide you to balance activity levels throughout the day and ensure there are periods of rest, reducing overall fatigue.

Adjusting the environment can have a huge impact on managing sundowning. Increasing lighting in the home as the day progresses can help minimize shadows and reduce confusion while supporting the sleep-wake cycle. Consider installing timers on lights so that no area within the living space suddenly becomes too dim, especially in the late afternoon and evening. Reducing background noise or playing soft, soothing music can provide a comforting background that helps ease the transition into the evening. These environmental tweaks don't require major renovations; small changes like additional lamps, reducing the volume on televisions and radios, and using blackout curtains to minimize confusing cues about the time of day can all be beneficial.

Engaging in calming activities in the evening can also serve as a gentle distraction and aid in reducing sundowning symptoms. Activities should be simple and soothing. For instance, looking through photo albums can be a wonderful way to connect and engage. This activity fosters interaction and fosters reminiscence, which can be comforting for someone experiencing memory loss. Alternatively, simple craft activities like coloring or assembling puzzles can also provide focus and a sense of accomplishment. The key is to choose activities that are relaxing and not overly stimulating, which could increase confusion or agitation. Here is a list of some activities that I researched and tried with my parents:

- Planting seeds
- Reading
- Playing card games
- Making a collage
- Playing with play dough
- Making PVC pipe figures

Try to vary the activities that you do in the afternoons because each can have different benefits. For example, reading can help with language skills, whereas planting seeds is good for fine motor skills. The main goal is to ensure your loved one enjoys engaging in activities, but that doesn't mean you should suffer in silence with activities that bore you. This is another good reason to explore different activities for both of you to take pleasure in together, which leads nicely to the importance of caring for yourself during sundowning.

As a caregiver, preparing yourself for the challenges of sundowning is just as important as preparing for the physical environment. Understanding that difficult evenings are possible can help you approach the situation with patience and compassion rather than frustration or surprise. Ensure you are well-rested and supported, as your state of mind can significantly influence how you manage evening challenges. Establishing a support network, whether through family, friends, or caregiver support groups, can provide you with the backup you need on particularly challenging days—don't worry; we will cover how to do this a little later. Remember, taking care of your emotional and physical well-being enables you to provide the best care for your loved one.

Managing sundowning effectively requires a blend of observation, environmental management, engaging activities, and caregiver preparation. Each evening might not be perfect, but with the right strategies, you can create a more predictable and soothing environment that eases the transition into the night for your loved one. As you continue to learn and adapt, remember that your efforts are creating a calmer, more nurturing space that supports both the well-being of your loved one and your own.

Safety Proofing Your Home for Dementia Patients

Creating a safe home environment is crucial when you're caring for someone with dementia. As their ability to navigate daily life diminishes, even the most familiar surroundings can become filled with potential hazards. You'll need to perform a thorough risk assessment. This involves walking through your home with a fresh perspective and identifying anything that could pose a risk to your loved one. To help you gain this new perspective, here is a safety checklist to use as you go through your loved one's home.

- Install handrails on both sides of stairways.
- Install handrails in baths and showers.
- Add glow-in-the-dark tape on the stairs.
- Install automatic sensory lights on stairs and other poorly lit areas.
- Put a nightlight near their bed.
- Remove clutter from hallways.
- Consider ramps for steps.

- Remove door mats and throw rugs.
- Secure larger furniture to prevent tipping over.
- Secure electrical wires and extension cables.
- Regularly check all smoke detectors and carbon monoxide detectors.
- Place cleaning products in a lockable cupboard.
- Keep medication and other potential hazards in lockable cupboards.
- Place textured stickers on slippery surfaces.
- Add temperature control faucets.
- Place things in cupboards and drawers so they are easy to reach.
- Consider an alarm system.
- Check outdoor fences and gates to ensure they are secure.
- Add stickers to panes of glass for clear visibility.
- Disconnect the garbage disposal.
- Install simple-to-use appliances with automatic shut-off.
- Consider disconnecting or removing potentially hazardous appliances like gas stoves.
- Remove toxic plants or any decorations that could be mistaken as edible.

There is no need to feel overwhelmed at the thought of doing this all at once. Safety-proofing the home is often a task that progresses along with the symptoms of dementia. Clutter and things that can cause a fall might be more of a priority early on, whereas temperature-controlled faucets may be a little extreme and even insulting for someone in the early stages of dementia.

Technology can also play a pivotal role in enhancing home safety. Motion sensors can alert you if your loved one is moving around the house at unusual times, which can be particularly useful for managing nocturnal wandering—a common and stressful aspect of dementia care. GPS tracking devices can be a lifesaver if your loved one leaves the house unnoticed. These devices can be attached to clothing or worn as a bracelet, allowing you to locate the person if they wander off quickly. It's also worth considering a dementia ID tag or bracelet that informs others of your loved one's condition in case they do wander off.

Regular safety reviews are essential as dementia progresses. The needs of your loved one will change over time, and what was once a safe environment can become problematic. For example, as mobility decreases, additional modifications, such as wheelchair ramps or stairlifts, might become necessary. Regularly walking through your home to reassess the environment ensures that you can adapt to new challenges, maintaining a safe and supportive space for your loved one to live in.

Taking proactive steps to assess and improve home safety creates a secure environment that supports your loved one's well-being and gives you peace of mind. Remember, these changes protect them from physical harm and help them maintain their independence for as long as possible, which is invaluable for their dignity and quality of life. As you continue to adapt your home and routines, you're building a safer, more nurturing space that respects their needs and challenges, making each day much easier and safer.

Navigating Nutritional Challenges: A Caregiver's Plan

One often overlooked but critical aspect of dementia care revolves around nutrition. As dementia progresses, your loved one might face a variety of eating challenges—from diminished appetite to forgetting meals or difficulties with chewing. My dad had to be reminded to eat. He was so skinny. My mom was quite the opposite. She was always hungry! These issues can drastically impact their health and well-being, making proper nutrition essential. It's not just about what they eat but how they can eat safely and enjoyably, maintaining as much independence as possible.

Additionally, motor and sensory difficulties can make the physical act of eating challenging. Then there's the matter of taste and smell—senses that often diminish with age, and more so in individuals with neurological conditions, potentially making food seem unappetizing (Anthem Memory Care 2018). Addressing these issues often starts with understanding these transformed needs and finding ways to meet them effectively. High-calorie, nutrient-dense foods can help ensure your loved ones get enough energy, even if their food intake has decreased. Smoothies and soups can be excellent options, providing the necessary nutrients in an easy-to-consume form. Moreover, maintaining a schedule for meals can help in establishing a routine that reminds them it's time to eat, which can be especially helpful if they struggle with memory loss.

When it comes to meal planning, incorporating preferences and nutritional needs is key to encouraging appetite and enjoyment. If your loved one has always liked a certain flavor or type of food, try including these in their diet. However, textures might need adjusting. If chewing or swallowing is an issue, consider softer food options or those that require minimal chewing, like mashed potatoes or casseroles. It's also helpful to prepare meals that are easy to eat independently, encouraging self-feeding for as long as possible, which once again considers their dignity. Preparing small, frequent meals rather than three large ones can also be beneficial, as it can be less overwhelming and helps ensure that they receive a steady intake of calories and nutrients throughout the day.

Hydration can be another challenge because your loved one forgets to drink or can't recognize signs of thirst. It's a good idea to offer a wide variety of drinks as well as water, including tea and coffee, fruit juices, and flavored water. Choose smaller cups or glasses so they aren't too heavy or awkward. Another fantastic idea is Jelly Drops, sweets that are sugar-free and 95 percent water with added electrolytes (Alzheimer's Society 2022).

Adaptive tools and techniques for eating can greatly assist individuals with dementia. Utensils with easy-grip handles or weighted options can help those with tremors or coordination issues, making it easier for them to feed themselves. Non-slip dishes can prevent accidents, and plates with high-contrast colors can help those with visual impairments distinguish the food from the plate, enhancing their ability to eat independently. These tools make eating easier and help the person stay in control of their meals, boosting their morale and interest in eating.

As with any aspect of dementia care, close monitoring and flexibility are crucial. Keep an eye on their nutritional intake and be ready to make adjustments as their health needs change. Weight loss or gain can indicate whether their dietary needs are being met. If you notice negative changes, it might be time to reassess your meal plan or consult with a healthcare professional like a dietitian who can provide specialized advice tailored to their needs. Regularly discussing these needs with your healthcare provider ensures that any medical conditions that could be influencing their appetite or digestion are managed properly.

Good nutrition, including hydration, supports overall health, improves mood, and enhances quality of life, making it a vital component of effective dementia care. As you adapt meals and methods to meet their changing needs, remember that these efforts are about maintaining physical health and nurturing their spirit through the simple pleasure of a good meal.

Exercise Plans for Dementia Patients: Boosting Physical and Mental Health

Embracing physical activity as a vital component of care for your loved one with dementia can bring a multitude of benefits that extend beyond mere physical health. Regular exercise has been shown to improve mobility, mood, and sleep patterns, which are often major areas of concern in dementia care. Studies have shown that physical activity isn't just a way to improve the quality of life for dementia patients. It also helps to lower the load of distress for caregivers (Sampaio et al., 2021).

Physical activity helps in maintaining and even improving mobility, which is crucial because it influences everything from independence in daily tasks to overall physical resilience. Furthermore, exercise releases endorphins, natural mood lifters, which can help alleviate some of the emotional challenges like depression and anxiety that often accompany dementia. Numerous studies have shown that regular exercise has a positive impact on mood, which is especially important when you consider that antidepressants are more likely to have adverse effects on older people with dementia (Williams & Tappen, 2008). Improved sleep is another significant benefit. Regular physical activity can help regulate sleep patterns, making it easier for your loved one to fall asleep and stay asleep throughout the night.

Creating tailored exercise routines that cater to the specific needs and abilities of your loved one is key. In the early stages of dementia, more active and engaging exercises can be very beneficial. Walking remains one of the simplest yet most effective forms of exercise. It doesn't require special equipment and can be easily adapted to the person's capabilities. Perhaps start with short walks around the neighborhood or in a local park, places that are familiar and not overly crowded. As the dementia progresses, you might need to shorten the duration of the walks or switch to quieter, more controlled environments.

Stretching is an especially good exercise because it keeps your loved one flexible and helps prevent injuries. Simple stretching exercises can be done at home with minimal supervision once they are familiar with the routine. Chair exercises are also excellent, especially for those with limited mobility. These can include seated marches, leg lifts, or even stretching the arms upwards, all movements that help maintain joint flexibility and muscle strength without the risk of falls. Don't think that these types of exercises are only beneficial for the elderly. Simple stretches and chair exercises are good for everyone, and what's more, it's a wonderful chance for you to do something together, motivate each other, and bond.

Incorporating social interaction into these exercise routines can significantly enhance their effectiveness and enjoyment. Consider group exercise classes designed specifically for seniors or individuals with cognitive impairments if possible. These classes provide an opportunity for social interaction, which can be both stimulating and comforting. Alternatively, engaging family members in exercise routines, like family walks, can turn physical activity into joyful family time, fostering emotional bonds and creating positive experiences for everyone involved. As my parents' dementia advanced, it was actually the younger grandchildren who got more of a response from them, which was lovely to see.

Safety and proper supervision are so important when implementing an exercise plan for someone with dementia. Always ensure that the environment where the exercise takes place is safe and free from hazards. It's important to pace the activities to match the current physical abilities of your loved one, recognizing that these might fluctuate from day to day. Always be present to guide and support them through each activity, ready to adjust the intensity as needed.

It's also advisable to consult with healthcare professionals, such as physiotherapists, who can help design a suitable exercise program and provide guidance on how to carry out the exercises safely. Another reason to look for specialized classes is that you have peace of mind that your loved one is with trained professionals, and you can take a break from caregiving.

Incorporating regular physical activity into the care routine for a loved one with dementia is essentially about enhancing their physical capabilities, however, it goes beyond that. It's a holistic approach that supports their emotional and mental well-being, enriches their social life, and improves overall quality of life. As you integrate these practices into your daily routine, remember that each small step contributes to a greater goal of maintaining dignity, joy, and health in your loved one's life.

As this chapter on practical caregiving strategies comes to an end, it's clear that each aspect, from daily routines to communication, safety, nutrition, and exercise, is interconnected and plays a crucial role in managing dementia effectively. Together, they form a comprehensive approach that not only addresses the immediate needs of your loved one but also anticipates future challenges, ensuring that you are prepared for every stage of the disease. As we move forward into the next chapter, we'll explore the legal and financial considerations in dementia care, providing you with the knowledge and tools to confidently navigate these complex areas.

Chapter 3

Legal and Financial Planning

L egal and financial planning can feel like an intimidating maze designed just to trip you up, especially when you are already dealing with the emotional weight of dementia caregiving. Maybe it's the paperwork, the legal jargon, or the sheer gravity of making decisions that can have long-lasting effects—whatever it is, you're not alone in feeling overwhelmed. When I first faced these tasks while caring for my parents, I wished for a guide to walk me through each step with clarity and understanding. That's exactly what this chapter aims to be for you—a clear, empathetic guide through the essential legal documents and planning needed in dementia care.

Essential Legal Documents for Dementia Caregiving

One of the first things that you may need to discuss with your loved one and other family members is the power of attorney. The term "power of attorney" (POA) can sound daunting, but it's fundamentally a tool for ensuring that someone you trust can make decisions on your behalf when you can no longer do so. In the context of dementia, setting up a POA for both financial and healthcare decisions is so important as the disease progresses. A financial POA will manage financial matters, from paying bills to managing estates and investments, while a healthcare POA will make decisions about medical treatments and health care (Alzheimer's Association, n.d.-a).

This legal document becomes effective based on the criteria specified within it—often when the individual cannot make competent decisions as certified by a medical professional. It's vital to choose someone who is trustworthy and capable of handling these responsibilities with your loved one's best interests at heart. I strongly advise you to do this as soon as possible and with a legal professional. If your loved one can't understand what power of attorney means, you will likely have to go to additional legal lengths and costs to be able to achieve this essential document.

Advanced Healthcare Directives, like living wills, are key parts of proactive legal planning. These documents allow your loved one to express their wishes regarding end-of-life care, ensuring that these preferences are respected even if they can no longer communicate them. A living will typically covers life-sustaining treatment scenarios and can specify which treatments your loved one would or would not want. It is typically known as a Physician Order for Life-Sustaining Treatment (Alzheimer's Association, n.d.-a). These directives alleviate the immense burden on family members who might otherwise have to make these difficult decisions under incredibly stressful and emotional circumstances. These decisions can be made harder when siblings or other family members disagree. It's about respecting your loved one's wishes and providing peace of mind to you and them, knowing that their values and preferences will guide critical healthcare decisions.

There may be a time when it becomes necessary to consider guardianship or conservatorship, as mentioned before, when someone is incapable of signing the power of attorney or other legal documents. These legal structures are designed to protect individuals who can no longer care for themselves or manage their finances. Guardianship gives a designated guardian legal authority to make personal decisions for the individual, while conservatorship relates specifically to managing the individual's finances (Alzheimer's Association, n.d.-a). Both require a court appointment, typically proving the individual's incapacity through medical testimony and a legal process. While these measures can provide essential protection, they also involve a significant legal and emotional undertaking, emphasizing the importance of discussing these options with a legal professional who can guide you through the complexities.

Once these documents are in place, managing them correctly is just as important. Ensure that all legal documents are stored securely and remain accessible when needed. A fireproof safe in your home can be a good option. Keeping copies with a trusted attorney and in a secure cloud storage service can ensure they are available even if you cannot access the originals. Ensure that the people who will need to use these documents—like the designated POA or healthcare proxy—know where they are stored and how to access them, ensuring that no administrative hurdles will delay necessary actions.

Managing these legal documents is more than something to tick off your to-do list. It's about protecting your loved one's wishes and rights. Think of it this way: Your loved ones have dedicated their lives to putting your best interests at heart; it's only fair we do the same. It's about making thoughtful, informed decisions that respect their dignity and ensure their well-being throughout the progression of dementia. The forms you fill out today will provide clarity and peace of mind for everyone involved.

Financial Planning: Managing Costs and Budgeting

Creating a sensible and thorough budget when caring for someone with dementia is like preparing for a journey with many unexpected turns. As you consider financial planning, remember it's about calculating immediate costs and anticipating future costs. Let's start with the nitty-gritty of setting up a budget that accounts for medical expenses, caregiving supplies, and potential home modifications.

Firstly, itemizing your current expenses is crucial. List everything from medications and medical appointments to daily caregiving supplies like incontinence products or nutritional supplements. Don't overlook the less obvious needs, such as transport costs to and from medical appointments. Each item on your list should be accompanied by an estimated cost, helping you form a clear picture of monthly expenditures.

Next, consider the living environment. Is a home modification necessary to ensure safety and accessibility? This might include installing grab bars in the bathroom, ramps for wheelchair access, or even more significant modifications like a stair lift. Are there funds available for these modifications, or will you need to take out a loan? If home improvements do need financing, their repayment will need to be included in the monthly expenses.

Creating a budget isn't just about tallying current costs—it's also planning for the future. Because dementia is a progressive condition, associated costs can increase over time. This is where long-term financial planning becomes essential. It's prudent to set aside resources for anticipated future needs, which might include professional in-home care or eventual transition to a residential care facility. Additionally, consider the potential costs for end-of-life care, respectfully discussing and planning in advance. This kind of forward-thinking financial planning helps prevent the stress of unexpected expenses, ensuring you can focus on providing care without constant financial worry.

Managing the daily financial tasks of a person with dementia presents its own set of challenges. As cognitive function declines, tasks like paying bills, managing bank accounts, and keeping track of expenses can become overwhelming. Implementing a system is crucial so you know that every aspect of your loved one's finances is handled efficiently. Setting up automatic payments for regular bills can reduce the burden and help avoid missed payments. Regularly reviewing bank statements can help you keep track of spending and spot any irregularities early, and it might also be worth setting up notifications if you have a busy schedule. It's also wise to simplify financial management wherever possible, perhaps consolidating accounts or reducing the number of credit cards to streamline monitoring and management.

The importance of financial professionals in this situation cannot be overstated. Financial advisors and planners who specialize in elder care can be invaluable. They bring their expertise in financial management and an understanding of the unique challenges posed by long-term care needs. These professionals can guide you in investment decisions so that funds are available and adequately allocated as needed over time. They can also help navigate the often-complex landscape of retirement funds, pensions, and other assets, making sure these are utilized in the most beneficial manner.

Involving a financial professional early in your planning can also provide peace of mind, knowing that you have a strategy in place to secure your loved one's financial well-being. They can offer advice tailored to your specific situation, helping you make informed decisions that protect and maximize your loved one's assets. Whether adjusting investment portfolios to suit better the need for liquidity or planning for tax implications related to care expenses, their guidance is indispensable.

I know you are going to be tempted to take the financial planning on yourself, especially if the situation appears quite straightforward. But even then, bear in mind that you are taking on an awful lot on top of your own responsibilities. It's not to say you aren't capable, but it's about knowing where best to direct your resources. If it's between an hour of stressing over finances or an hour of making your loved one smile, you know what you need to be doing. You are already a hero by taking care of them; you don't need to do it all!

As you tackle the financial planning needed for dementia care, remember that each decision you make, from the daily management of finances to long-term planning, is about working toward stability and security. By taking a detailed, proactive approach to budgeting and financial management, you set a foundation that supports the ongoing care and well-being of your loved one, allowing you to focus more on the moments you share rather than the costs they entail.

Understanding and Applying for Government Aid

It's great that there is financial support available, but boy, they don't make it easy. I spent so much time trying to get all the help I could for my parents. I had yet to learn how to do it or exactly what they even qualified for. Understanding and accessing these resources can provide significant financial relief and support. Let's break down the maze of available government programs, their eligibility criteria, and how to maximize the benefits to ensure your loved one receives every possible advantage.

The U.S. government provides several programs that can help manage the costs associated with dementia care. Medicaid, for instance, is pivotal for many families. It's not just for those with low income but also offers benefits for long-term care, which can cover both in-home and nursing home care for individuals with dementia. Some memory care services that are covered by Medicaid include twenty-four-hour supervision and nursing care, physical activities, and physical, occupational, and speech therapies (The National Council on Aging, 2023). The eligibility for Medicaid can vary by state, but generally, it requires meeting specific income and asset criteria.

Social Security Disability Income (SSDI) is another crucial program, especially if dementia has led to early retirement or the inability to work. SSDI benefits are based on the recipient's previous work credits and payroll tax contributions, providing a monthly income for those who qualify (Laurence, 2024). For veterans, the VA Aid and Attendance benefit is a godsend, offering additional monetary assistance to those who require the aid and attendance of another person due to physical disabilities. This can include individuals with advanced dementia who need regular supervision (VeteranAid, 2018).

Applying for these programs involves a series of steps that can initially seem daunting. Each program has its own set of forms, documentation requirements, and often a lengthy review process. For Medicaid, the application is usually made through state Medicaid offices, where you'll need to provide detailed financial records and evidence of medical necessity, which, in the case of dementia, includes a comprehensive diagnosis from a healthcare provider. For SSDI, applications can be submitted online, but they require thorough medical records and documentation proving that the dementia is severe enough to prevent any gainful employment. The VA's Aid and Attendance benefit also requires proof of the need for daily assistance, verified through medical evaluation forms.

To maximize the benefits of these programs, it's essential to present a well-prepared case. This means gathering comprehensive documentation that proves the diagnosis, outlines the required care level, and clearly demonstrates the financial need. Detailed medical records, doctor's notes, and a daily care journal can be instrumental in painting a full picture of the individual's condition and needs. Additionally, consulting with professionals such as eldercare lawyers or financial advisors specializing in care planning can provide invaluable guidance and help streamline the application process, ensuring you present the strongest case possible.

The process of applying for financial aid may take time, so a little patience goes a long way, and it's another one of those tasks that should be started as soon as possible. Furthermore, as symptoms worsen, it's essential to request reassessments if more funding is available.

State-specific programs also play a crucial role in supporting dementia care. Many states offer supplemental programs that can help cover costs related to prescriptions, medical care, and even respite care for caregivers. These programs can vary widely in terms of what they offer and who qualifies, so it's important to contact local aging agencies or Medicaid offices to find out what's available in your area. They often have counselors who specialize in elder care benefits and can offer guidance tailored to your specific situation. It's worth contacting the Alzheimer's Association for state-specific information.

As you apply for these programs, remember that persistence is key. The bureaucracy can be frustrating, and applications may sometimes be denied initially, requiring appeals and additional documentation. Staying organized, keeping detailed records, and seeking support from professionals can help manage this process more effectively, ensuring that you and your loved ones are getting the support you need. With careful planning, detailed documentation, and a little perseverance, you can access these benefits, securing much-needed support that significantly eases the extensive costs of long-term dementia care.

I can't stress enough the importance of early legal and financial planning. My parents did not have a lot of money, but they still had a home. I fought my dad for a good while, trying to take over their finances and get them set up for the long journey that was ahead of us. Know the laws in your state and get legal and financial advice early. I think that was one of the most draining parts of my caregiving journey. We sold everything and used that money for their care, and then my siblings and I had to take over the financial burden. We would have had access to so many more resources if we had just started working on things earlier.

Insurance: Claims, Coverage, and Confusions

Dealing with insurance means you will be faced with a myriad of terms, policies, and types of insurance that all seem crucially important but incredibly complex. Understanding the basic types of insurance that are most relevant to dementia care is the first step. Health insurance is the most familiar, covering medical expenses like doctor visits, hospital stays, and, in some cases, certain types of long-term care.

Long-term care insurance, on the other hand, specifically helps cover the cost of chronic medical conditions, including the day-to-day care that dementia patients often require, such as assistance with personal care and supervision. There are two main categories of long-term care insurance (LTC insurance): traditional and hybrid. Traditional LTC insurance covers long-term care, whereas hybrid LTC insurance combines long-term care with life insurance (National Council on Aging 2023-b). Life insurance, while not directly covering care costs, can offer financial relief to families after a loved one has passed, which can be instrumental in settling final expenses and outstanding medical bills.

Filing insurance claims and managing the inevitable denials that sometimes follow can seem intimidating. It's important to approach this aspect with a clear, organized mindset. When filing a claim, ensure you have all the documentation readily available. This includes medical records that clearly outline the necessity for the care provided, as well as detailed receipts and invoices. Most insurance companies have specific forms and processes for filing claims, so following these guidelines precisely is crucial to avoid unnecessary delays or denials.

Nevertheless, denials can still happen and can be based on a range of issues, from a simple clerical error to a discrepancy in policy coverage interpretation. When faced with a denial, carefully review the insurer's explanation and prepare to appeal the decision. This process typically involves submitting a formal appeal letter and any additional documentation supporting the case for coverage. It's a process where persistence and attention to detail can make a significant difference.

Understanding the often-complex language of insurance policies is helpful. Terms like "deductible," "premium," "co-payment," and "out-of-pocket maximum" are not just jargon; they are critical components of how much you will end up paying for care. For instance, a deductible is the amount you pay before your insurance starts to pay its share for covered services. A premium, on the other hand, is the regular payment you make to keep the insurance active (DISB, n.d.). Knowing these terms helps you better understand what is covered and your financial responsibilities under the policy. This knowledge empowers you to make informed decisions about care and coverage.

Regular reviews of your insurance coverage are essential, especially as the care needs of someone with dementia can change rapidly. What was sufficient coverage at one stage may become inadequate as their condition progresses and care needs increase. Schedule regular check-ins on your policies to ensure the coverage meets your needs. This might mean increasing the benefit amount on a long-term care policy or adjusting a health insurance plan to reduce out-of-pocket expenses. Adjustments might also include adding supplementary policies to cover aspects not included in your current plans. Keeping your insurance coverage aligned with care needs helps manage your financial risk and prevents unexpected expenses from overwhelming resources.

Estate Planning and Dementia: A Detailed Guide

Estate planning might bring images of lawyers and stacks of paperwork to mind, but at its heart, it's about ensuring that your loved one's wishes are honored and that their affairs are in order, no matter what the future holds. When you're dealing with a diagnosis of dementia, these considerations become even more pressing. The basic components of estate planning—wills, trusts, and beneficiary designations—form the backbone of ensuring that your loved one's assets are managed and distributed according to their wishes after they pass away.

A will is essential; it dictates how assets should be distributed and can designate guardians for any dependents. Trusts can be used to manage assets during the individual's lifetime and beyond, offering control over how and when assets are distributed. Beneficiary designations, meanwhile, are essential for policies and accounts like life insurance or retirement funds, ensuring that these assets go directly to the chosen beneficiaries without passing through probate.

If we delve a little deeper into wills and beneficiary designations, there is one fundamental difference that cannot be overlooked. A will can be contested, meaning family members, if they choose, can go to probate court if they disagree—even family not listed on a will. On the other hand, contracts with financial institutions state an unquestionable beneficiary and can't be overruled by family members. For example, if your loved one states on their will that they want their $401,000 to go to a child, but the beneficiary is a sibling, the $401,000 will go to the sibling (Kilroy, 2023). It's these types of details that can be easily missed but can have serious implications.

The progression of dementia adds a layer of complexity to these already intricate planning processes. As cognitive abilities decline, the capacity to make legal decisions can become compromised. This makes early planning essential—not just preferable. The legal standard for mental capacity can vary, but generally, it requires that the individual understands the implications of their decisions. Setting up estate plans early in the diagnosis ensures that you and your loved one are not caught in a situation where the ability to make these decisions is in question. It also prevents potential legal challenges to the decisions made later due to questions about capacity. Personally, I found it made sense to do all the estate planning at the same time as the power of attorney.

Special Needs Trusts (SNTs) offer a unique tool in estate planning for families managing dementia care. These trusts can hold assets for the benefit of an individual with dementia without disqualifying them from receiving means-tested government benefits like Medicaid (Young, 2024). This is crucial because direct inheritance could disqualify your loved one from these benefits, potentially disrupting their care continuity. An SNT allows you to set aside funds that can enhance the quality of life for your loved one, covering costs that go beyond basic needs, such as personal care attendants, out-of-pocket medical expenses, or even leisure activities. However, setting up an SNT requires careful consideration and precise drafting to ensure compliance with legal standards, so it's advisable to work with an attorney experienced in this area.

Involving family members in the estate planning process is vital, yet it can be a source of tension and conflict. Transparent, open communication is key to ensuring all parties understand the plans and the reasons behind specific decisions. Start these conversations early and involve all relevant family members. Be clear about your loved one's wishes and the plans to honor them. You can have these discussions in the presence of the legal advisor, who can help clarify any legal nuances and mediate any disagreements.

Documenting these discussions can also be helpful, as well as a reference to avoid future misunderstandings. Despite the sense of urgency, if things do get heated with family members, know that it's okay to walk away, let things calm down, and go back to the conversation later. There are a lot of extremely intense emotions flying around, and that's not the right moment to have such conversations. Remember, the goal of involving family members isn't just to inform but to foster cohesion and support around the shared objective of caring for your loved one.

Estate planning in the context of dementia requires a delicate balance of legal knowledge, timely action, and family dynamics. By understanding the fundamental elements and engaging with them proactively, you are taking the necessary steps so that your loved one's legacy is protected and that their wishes are respected, all while maintaining eligibility for crucial benefits and fostering family harmony.

Fraud Protection and Scam Awareness for Caregivers

In the world of dementia care, where much focus is rightly placed on physical and emotional well-being, the financial safety of our loved ones often becomes a secondary concern. However, the unfortunate reality is that elderly individuals, particularly those with cognitive impairments like dementia, are prime targets for scams and fraudulent schemes. Statistics show that in 2022 alone, over 80,000 people aged sixty and over were the victims of financial scams, and this equated to $3.1 billion (K2 Medical Research, n.d.).

Recognizing common scams, arming yourself with preventive measures, and knowing the steps to take if an incident occurs are crucial components of comprehensive dementia care. Before we get into intentional financial scams, there is also the risk of unintentional scams. I remember talking to a woman in a support group whose mom had answered the phone to several companies who were asking people if they wanted to sign up for magazine subscriptions. All calls were genuine because before the woman knew what had happened, there were twenty magazines arriving at her mom's home each month. This highlights the importance of managing access to bank cards, especially credit cards.

Scammers often exploit the vulnerabilities of the elderly, utilizing tactics that range from posing as representatives from legitimate companies or government organizations to creating fake charities or investment opportunities. One common scam involves the "grandparent scam," where the scammer pretends to be a grandchild in distress, urgently needing money for an emergency (Ravichandran, 2023). Another frequent tactic is the "utility scam," in which the perpetrator claims to be a utility worker demanding immediate payment for a supposed overdue bill, threatening to cut off the service (Segura, 2024). These scams can be particularly convincing and devastating as they prey on the victims' emotions and sense of urgency.

Protecting your loved one from such scams starts with awareness and education. First, please make sure that all caregivers and family members understand the risk and are familiar with the most common scams. Open communication about these risks can help build a protective network around your loved one. It's also vital to safeguard personal information diligently. This includes shredding documents with personal information before disposal, securing sensitive information like social security numbers or bank account details, and ensuring that digital data is protected with strong, regularly updated passwords. Frequently reviewing bank and credit card statements to spot unusual activity is important as well. Setting up alerts for new transactions can also provide immediate updates on financial activity, allowing for quicker action if something suspicious appears.

If you suspect that your loved one has been targeted by a scam, acting swiftly can alleviate the damage. Start by documenting everything related to the incident, including the date, time, description of the interaction, and any contact information provided by the scammer. This documentation is very important when reporting the incident to authorities. Contact the local police and consider filing a report with the Federal Trade Commission (FTC) through their website. For financial scams, alert the financial institutions involved immediately to place holds on accounts and prevent further unauthorized access.

Educational resources and support networks play a pivotal role in both prevention and recovery. Organizations like the American Association of Retired Persons (AARP) offer extensive resources on current scams and prevention tips. They also provide support for scam victims, helping them navigate the aftermath of fraud. Local community centers or senior organizations often host workshops and talks on fraud prevention specifically tailored to older adults, which can be invaluable in keeping up to date with the latest scam tactics and protective measures.

By prioritizing scam awareness and prevention as part of your caregiving strategy, you protect your loved one's finances and contribute to their overall sense of security and dignity. This proactive approach ensures that their well-being is safeguarded on all fronts, allowing them to focus more on enjoying life despite the challenges of dementia.

As we conclude this chapter on legal and financial planning, we've covered a range of critical areas, from securing essential legal documents to understanding insurance and government aid and protecting against fraud. Each segment of this chapter provides you with tools and knowledge to manage the complex legal and financial landscape of dementia care effectively.

Moving onto the next chapter, we will explore building and utilizing support networks. Trust me, this is something that you won't appreciate, and how much it can help until it is in place.

Chapter 4

Building and Utilizing Support Networks

Despite having numerous medical appointments on top of everything else you have to do, caregiving can be incredibly isolating. I found that after watching my parents struggle, how could I talk to others about what I was going through? Regardless how emotionally strong and determined you are, caregiving takes a village. A support network is there to offer you comfort and reassurance as well as offer new perspectives and even skills. It's not easy finding your support group but with a little guidance, it's more than possible.

Crafting Your Personal Caregiving Team

The first step in assembling your caregiving team is identifying potential members. This group might include family members, friends, neighbors, or even members of your community who have expressed a desire to help. Start by listing everyone who has shown concern or offered assistance. Remember, including various individuals can bring diverse skills and availability, enriching the care provided. For instance, a neighbor might not be able to assist with personal care but could help with grocery shopping or yard work. Similarly, a friend who is a nurse or has medical experience can be invaluable for managing health-related tasks. Consider each person's strengths and how these can best support your caregiving needs, creating a well-rounded team that can adapt to various challenges.

Once you have identified potential team members, the next crucial step is defining roles and responsibilities. This clarity prevents overlap and ensures that all caregiving aspects are covered. For example, one person could be responsible for managing medical appointments, another for handling meal preparation, and another could manage finances or legal matters. It's important to have open discussions with each team member about what tasks they are comfortable taking on so that each member's boundaries and capabilities are respected. Regular meetings or digital check-ins can help reassess role assignments and adjust based on evolving needs or changes in availability.

Effective communication is the glue that holds your caregiving team together. Establishing clear and open communication channels enables everyone to remain informed, and care is coordinated efficiently. Consider setting up a group chat via text or a dedicated app where updates can be shared quickly. Regular meetings, either in person or via video calls, can be beneficial for more detailed discussions. During these meetings, discuss the current care strategies, any changes in your loved one's condition, and any adjustments needed in the caregiving plan. Tools, like shared online calendars or scheduling apps, can also be incredibly helpful in coordinating tasks and appointments so that everyone is on the same page.

Even with the best intentions, conflicts can arise within your caregiving team. Different opinions on care strategies or misunderstandings over roles can create tension. Handling these conflicts constructively is essential to maintaining a harmonious team dynamic. I know as the primary caregiver, there were quite a few moments when I felt others didn't know what they were talking about because I was with my parents the most. Unfortunately, this just meant I was ignoring perspectives that could have made my parents' lives easier and more enjoyable. If you are struggling with people who are somewhat controlling like me, it's a good idea to print off information you find or send links with a simple, "Saw this and thought it was an interesting read." It might be better received than telling someone what they should be doing.

When a disagreement occurs, address it promptly. Provide a platform where each party can express their concerns without judgment. Often, conflicts arise from miscommunications or differing expectations, which can be resolved through open dialogue. Don't hesitate to revisit and clarify roles and responsibilities, or consider bringing in a neutral third party, like a social worker or a professional mediator, to help navigate more complex disputes. Remember, the goal is to foster a supportive environment focused on the best care for your loved one, not to win arguments.

Building and utilizing a support network effectively multiplies your strength and resilience as a caregiver. Each team member brings unique skills and perspectives, easing the burden and enriching the care provided. As you move forward, remember that it's not just about managing tasks but about nurturing relationships within the team and with your loved one.

Community Resources Every Caregiver Should Know

Have you seen those 5,000-piece puzzles of the night sky? It's like sitting in front of a sea of pieces with no clue where to start. Luckily, numerous community resources can help you fit these pieces together, offering support, education, and practical assistance to lighten your load and enrich your caregiving experience. Local Alzheimer's Associations, senior centers, public health services, and educational workshops are just a few of the gems in this treasure chest of community support. Diving into these resources connects you with others on similar paths and provides you with tools and knowledge that can transform your approach to caregiving.

Local chapters of the Alzheimer's Association and similar groups are invaluable allies. These organizations are dedicated to providing support and advancing research and education on dementia. Engaging with a local chapter can connect you with a wealth of resources, including support groups where you can share experiences and strategies with fellow caregivers. These groups often serve as a safe space for expressing feelings and challenges and a place where you won't be judged for venting your frustrations. Additionally, these organizations frequently offer educational programs that can help you understand the latest in dementia care practices and research, empowering you with the knowledge to better care for your loved one. To connect with these resources, you can start by visiting their websites or calling them; they often have community liaisons who can guide you to the services that best suit your needs.

Senior centers and adult day care programs offer more than just activities for your loved one; they provide vital socialization opportunities that can significantly enhance their quality of life. Engaging with peers in a structured setting can help maintain cognitive functions and emotional health, offering a sense of community and belonging that dementia might otherwise erode. For you, as a caregiver, these programs offer the dual benefit of respite—time that you can use to rest, handle personal affairs, or recharge. This break is crucial in preventing caregiver burnout, a common risk when the demands of caregiving become over-whelming. Many of these centers include programs specifically designed for dementia patients, ensuring that activities are suit-able and beneficial. You can find these programs through local community boards, online searches, or by asking healthcare providers for recommendations.

Public health and social services also play a critical role in supporting your caregiving journey. Many local health depart-ments offer programs that cater specifically to the needs of elderly citizens, including those with dementia. These services might include meal delivery programs for when cooking daily meals becomes too burdensome or transportation services that can help you manage medical appointments. Home health care services can also be arranged, providing professional assistance with health care needs right at your doorstep. These services can support the physical health of your loved one as well as help you manage the logistical challenges that can accompany caregiving. Accessing these services usually involves contacting your local health department or social services office to inquire about avail-able programs and eligibility requirements.

Lastly, participating in educational workshops and seminars is a sure way to build skills and knowledge while you connect with others. Healthcare institutions, community centers, and care-giving organizations may offer these educational opportunities.

They can range from practical workshops on caregiving techniques and first aid to seminars on legal and financial planning for caregivers. Engaging in these educational opportunities prepares you to handle the complexities of dementia but also keeps you informed about advancements and resources that can aid in your caregiving role. Many of these programs also provide certificates or other forms of recognition that can be helpful if you seek to formalize your role as a caregiver or expand your professional qualifications in the future. To find these workshops and seminars, watch community bulletins, visit local library boards, or check the offerings at community colleges and senior centers.

Professional Help: When to Call and What to Expect

There comes a point in the caregiving process when you might feel overwhelmed or notice that your loved one's needs have evolved beyond what can be managed at home. It's crucial to recognize when to seek professional help for the well-being of your loved one. You also have to think about preserving your own health and your effectiveness as a caregiver. Identifying the need for professional assistance often revolves around significant changes in the patient's health—such as increased frequency of falls, unmanageable behavioral changes, or a noticeable decline in cognitive functions. As a caregiver, if you find yourself constantly exhausted, experiencing health issues, or feeling emotionally drained, these are clear indicators that it's time to reach out for professional support.

Professional help can come from a variety of sources, each offering different types of support. Geriatricians specialize in the care of older adults and can oversee and coordinate the treatment of various health issues related to aging, including dementia. They are excellent at seeing the bigger picture of your loved one's health rather than focusing on one specialty. An example of this is medication. Geriatricians are extremely knowledgeable about drug side effects, so if your loved one is taking medication for various conditions, they can offer the best advice to avoid complications. Part of their role is also coordinating with a team of medical professionals, which can help you when neurologists or psychologists are involved in the care (Johns Hopkins Medicine 2021).

Being well-prepared can make a significant difference when appointments with these professionals approach. Start by gathering all necessary medical records, a list of medications, dietary information, and any previous diagnosis or treatments. It's also helpful to prepare a list of symptoms or changes you've observed and any specific incidents that highlight your concerns. Questions to ask might include the implications of any new symptoms, potential side effects of prescribed medications, or recommendations for managing daily dementia-related challenges. Keeping a dedicated notebook or digital document for this purpose can help you organize this information effectively, ensuring you have all pertinent details at your fingertips during appointments.

Building and maintaining productive relationships with health-care providers is another crucial element. Always approach interactions with doctors, nurses, and other health professionals with respect and openness, ready to discuss your concerns and listen to their professional advice. Effective communication can help establish a partnership where your insights as a caregiver are valued and the professional's expertise is leveraged to provide the best care. Regular updates about your loved one's condition and being proactive in discussing any concerns can foster ongoing support and continuity of care. Remember, these professionals are your allies in the caregiving process, and working closely with them can provide you with additional support and resources necessary to manage the complexities of dementia care.

Recognizing when to seek help and effectively engaging with professionals are crucial steps in ensuring comprehensive care for your loved one and support for yourself as a caregiver. It's a chance for you to address immediate health concerns and build a sustainable approach to managing dementia that incorporates expert insights and targeted interventions.

Online Support Networks and How to Engage Them

In the digital age, finding a community isn't restricted to your geographic location. Online support networks offer a lifeline not limited to physical boundaries, providing support and information at any time of the day, which is especially valuable in the unpredictable journey of dementia caregiving. Imagine having access to a global network of caregivers who understand exactly what you're going through at the click of a button.

The advantages of engaging with online communities are manifold. The most immediate benefit is the 24/7 accessibility. Whether it's late at night after a tough day or early in the morning before your day begins, these resources are just a few clicks away, ready to offer advice, a listening ear, or answers to your urgent questions. Moreover, these communities bring together caregivers from all walks of life and parts of the world, each with their own experiences and perspectives. This diversity can be incredibly enriching, offering a range of strategies and solutions that you might not find in your immediate environment. Online forums and social media groups dedicated to dementia care can provide support that is both empathetic and practical, helping to reduce the isolation that often accompanies caregiving.

To find the right online support, start by looking for forums and social media groups specifically focused on dementia care. Reputable organizations like the Alzheimer's Association often host their own online communities, which can be a good starting point. Additionally, platforms like Facebook and Reddit host various caregiving groups where members share experiences and advice. When choosing a group, take the time to read through posts and observe the interactions to ensure that the environment is a positive one. It's one thing to release your pent-up tension; it's another to be negative all the time, and you don't need people like that draining you of your energy. Look for groups that have active moderators who facilitate respectful and informative discussions. It's also wise to check how information is sourced and shared within the group to ensure credible advice.

Engaging effectively in these online communities involves a few key practices. Protecting your and your loved one's personal information is paramount. Be cautious about sharing sensitive details, and consider adjusting your privacy settings to control who can see your posts and personal information. When participating in discussions, it's important to respect other members' diverse opinions and experiences. Online interactions can sometimes be misinterpreted due to the lack of non-verbal cues; always communicate clearly and kindly. If you encounter conflicting advice, take the time to do your research or consult a healthcare professional before making any changes to care routines or treatments.

Leveraging online resources extends beyond social interaction and support—it also includes utilizing educational materials that can enhance your caregiving skills. Many online communities offer access to webinars, e-books, and expert blogs that cover a wide range of topics related to dementia care. These resources can provide deeper insights into the medical, legal (especially when it comes to state-specific information), and emotional aspects of caregiving, often featuring advice from specialists and experts in the field.

Respite Care: Finding and Using Short-term Relief

Many people fall into the habit of assuming respite care is a luxury when in fact it's essential for your health and your effectiveness as a career, ensuring you are step away from your role as a caregiver to rest and recharge. When you're refreshed, you're more present and effective, directly benefiting the loved one you care for, and it can reduce those snappy moments when stress is just too much. It's helpful to understand respite care not as a service you use when you're at your limit but as a regular part of your caregiving strategy that ensures your health and energy levels are maintained.

Several types of respite care services are available, each designed to fit different needs and situations. In-home respite care services bring a caregiver into your home to provide care while you take a break. This option can be particularly comforting to your loved one since they can stay in their familiar environment. Alternatively, adult day care centers offer a safe environment where your loved one can interact with others while engaging in structured activities, providing a stimulating social environment that benefits their cognitive and emotional health. Short-term residential stays in assisted living facilities or nursing homes can provide comprehensive care for longer breaks, such as family vacations or extended rest periods (Wayne et al., 2024). These facilities are equipped to handle the needs of dementia patients, offering professional supervision and care around the clock.

Finding the right respite care involves several practical steps. Start by assessing your needs and the needs of your loved one. Consider how often you need a break, the level of care your loved one requires, and your budget. Once you clearly understand your needs, begin researching local services. Contacting local Alzheimer's associations, visiting senior centers, or searching online can provide you with a list of providers. Don't hesitate to ask for recommendations from other caregivers or healthcare professionals who can offer insights based on their experiences.

When choosing a respite care service, consider both cost and quality. While budget is an important factor, the quality of care is paramount. Visit potential facilities, meet with staff, and check reviews from other users to gauge the quality of care. Check that the providers are trained to handle the specific needs of dementia patients and more specifically, any other health concerns your loved one has. For in-home services, request interviews with potential caregivers to ensure they are a good fit with your loved one. It's also wise to start with short trial periods to see how your loved one responds to the caregiver or the environment, allowing you to make adjustments before committing to longer periods. Here are some general things to keep in mind when choosing respite care:

- How are care providers screened?
- What are the staff's levels of training, qualifications, and experience?
- What's included in the program (transport, meals, activities)?
- How many hours of care are available?
- What is their procedure in case of an emergency?
- Does the provider have any specific requirements?
- What is the staff-to-residents ratio?

Making the most of respite care means ensuring a smooth transition for you and your loved one. Prepare your loved one in advance by discussing the plan with them, using simple and reassuring language. Leave detailed care instructions with the respite caregiver, including information about daily routines, dietary restrictions, medication schedules, and how to manage potential behavioral issues. Preparing a list of emergency contacts and instructions for handling unexpected situations is also helpful.

For your part, plan how you will use the respite time. Whether it's catching up on sleep, enjoying hobbies, or spending time with friends and family, make sure it's truly restorative for you. I know you will feel like you need to rush around and take care of a million other responsibilities, but please try to carve out time for you, too. Now is a good moment to brush up on your delegation skills and get other people involved in household chores that you don't need to be doing. Don't see respite care as a luxury; treat it as a necessity.

Therapeutic Interventions and When to Consider Them

Exploring therapeutic interventions can open up a world of beneficial possibilities for those under your care with dementia. Therapies such as music therapy, art therapy, and pet therapy are strategic tools that can improve the quality of life for your loved one. Each of these therapies brings unique benefits, often tapping into the remaining strengths and abilities of the person with dementia, providing comfort, and even reawakening parts of their personality that seemed lost.

Music therapy, for instance, is not just about listening to music. It involves active engagement, whether singing, playing simple instruments, or just clapping along to the rhythm. This form of therapy can be particularly powerful because musical memory is often preserved in people with dementia, even when other memories may be fading (Devere, 2017). Familiar tunes can evoke memories, improve mood, and provide a sense of continuity in their lives. Moreover, music can stimulate emotional and cognitive responses, enhance mental processes, and calm the mind, reducing anxiety and agitation (Dementia UK, 2023).

Art therapy offers a different palette of benefits. It allows expression in a way that words cannot, which is valuable when verbal communication becomes challenging. Handling different textures and colors and engaging in the act of creating can help improve motor skills and promote self-expression (Lesley University, n.d.). This process can be profoundly satisfying for someone who struggles with the frustrations that come with language loss. The act of creating something tangible can also boost self-esteem and provide a sense of accomplishment and joy.

Pet therapy is another area that has shown great promise in dementia care. Interactions with animals can lower stress, reduce blood pressure and heart rate, and provide a comforting presence that can reduce behavioral issues like wandering or agitation. Animals have a unique way of offering unconditional acceptance, making them perfect companions for those whose cognitive abilities might be in decline. The tactile stimulation of petting a dog or cat can also be soothing and can enhance motor skills and encourage physical activity (Woffindin, 2023).

Integrating these therapeutic interventions into daily life is about tailoring these therapies to the interests and abilities of the person with dementia. It involves observing their reactions and adapting the activities accordingly. For instance, if a particular type of music seems to trigger positive reactions, you might plan more activities around that genre or involve instruments that allow the person to participate actively. However, if you see an upsetting reaction, you know it's something to avoid. Similarly, art projects should be adapted to their skill level, ensuring they are simple enough to avoid frustration but challenging enough to provide a sense of achievement.

It's highly recommended to consult professionals who specialize in therapeutic interventions for dementia. Occupational therapists, for instance, can provide valuable insights into which activities are most suitable and how to adapt them to the individual's changing abilities. They can also offer guidance on safely implementing these activities, ensuring that the person with dementia gets the maximum benefit without risk of harm. Other roles of an occupational therapist can include working on communication, motor, and cognitive skills and strategies to work on short-term memory (Ferguson, 2023).

These therapeutic interventions are vital components of a holistic care strategy that addresses the physical, emotional, and psychological well-being of people with dementia. As we move onto the next chapter, we will delve into advanced caregiving topics, where we will explore more specialized care strategies and interventions so that you are well-equipped to handle the evolving challenges of dementia caregiving. This knowledge will prepare you for future needs and enhance your ability to provide compassionate, effective care as your loved one's journey progresses.

Help transform someone's darkness into light

"Sometimes it takes more courage to ask for help than to act alone."

— Ken Petti

Caring for someone with dementia can be an immensely isolating experience for many. Sure, friends and family may be kind and empathetic, but it often feels like few understand the many sleepless nights, worries, or moments of connection you experience when you are the main caregiver of a person with dementia. Symptoms of dementia in a loved one can creep up silently and slowly. Your loved one may forget a date or an experience you shared one day, and weeks down the line, they may fail to remember a loved one's name or significant life event. As their caregiver, you are the one noticing these changes and grieving the loss of a cherished memory. You are the one noticing changes in everyday functions and looking for creative ways to make things better.

By this stage in your reading, I hope you are feeling more accompanied and understood. After getting the practical matters out of the way (including safety-proofing your loved one's surroundings, rising to nutritional challenges, and working through legal and financial issues), I hope you are finding ways to make your own life better too. In the last chapter, you saw how crafting a support team is the first step toward balancing your loved one's needs with your own health and well-being. In the remaining chapters of the book, I will offer many more strategies for enhancing the quality of life of every member of your home. Before you progress further, however, I hope I can ask you for a small favor. Please share your opinion of this book with others.

By leaving a review of this book on Amazon, you'll help other caregivers strike the perfect balance between caring for their loved ones and building a fulfilling life for themselves.

Thanks for your support. I hope the rest of this book empowers you to weather the changes and developments that arise when you care for someone with dementia.

Chapter 5

Addressing Caregiver Health and Well-being

I magine you're in a plane, and the oxygen masks drop down in front of you. What's the first instruction always given? "Put on your own mask before helping others." This is not just vital in emergencies but also a metaphor for life, particularly when you're caring for someone with dementia. The role of a caregiver is immensely rewarding yet equally demanding. It's easy to lose yourself in the process of caring for someone else. This chapter is dedicated to you, the caregiver, focusing on essential self-care strategies that sustain your well-being while you provide care.

Self-Care Strategies for the Dementia Caregiver

Taking care of your health might seem like just another item on an endless to-do list, but it's the bedrock on which effective caregiving rests. Statistics show that caregivers are more likely to suffer from anxiety, depression, and other chronic health conditions (Family Caregiver Alliance, n.d.). Self-care can feel like you are prioritizing your own needs over the needs of others, and this is essentially true, but it's not selfish. There is a huge misconception that self-care is about taking yourself off for a day at the spa, and although this can be part of self-care if you feel the need, self-care isn't synonymous with luxury. On that note, let's cover the fundamentals of self-care.

Your Medical Health

Regular medical check-ups are non-negotiable; they ensure you remain physically capable of providing care. Just as important are your daily health routines. Whether taking medication, managing a balanced diet, or ensuring you're getting enough sleep, maintaining your health should be at the top of your priorities. There is no way around this—when your body is run down, the quality of care you provide will inevitably suffer. Plus, staying healthy sets a positive example for the person you care for as well as other family members, showing them the importance of health maintenance.

Setting Boundaries

Learning to set boundaries is perhaps one of the most challenging yet vital skills you need as a caregiver. It's easy to feel like you have to do everything by yourself, but setting limits is essential for long-term sustainability. This might mean defining what you can and cannot do in a day, learning to say no, or asking for help when the load gets too heavy. Remember, setting boundaries isn't a sign of weakness but a strategy for strength. It protects you from burnout and protects your mental well-being. A 2018 study showed that well-defined boundaries reduce levels of stress and anxiety (Turco, 2024).

Start by evaluating your weekly tasks and identify at least one activity you can delegate to someone else or eliminate altogether. Boundaries need to apply to all areas of life. You may need to set stronger boundaries around your work commitments. Above all, you will need to set time boundaries. It's easy to let others make plans that involve you, but in your mind, there are a dozen other things you would rather be doing. Regarding time boundaries, try to schedule time for yourself—even if it's just five or ten minutes here and there.

Taking Regular Breaks

Regular breaks throughout your day are vital intervals that allow you to recharge and return to caregiving with renewed energy and perspective. Even short breaks can significantly reduce stress levels, whether it's stepping outside for fresh air, enjoying a cup of tea, or simply sitting down to read a few pages of your favorite book. These moments of respite can help prevent feelings of resentment and exhaustion. Plan these breaks as diligently as you schedule medical appointments—they are just as important. If finding time is challenging, start small with five-minute intervals a few times a day, gradually increasing as you find the rhythm that works best for you.

Engaging in Enjoyable Activities

Lastly, it's crucial to engage in activities that bring you joy, separate from your caregiving duties. These activities help maintain your identity beyond being a caregiver and are key to managing stress. Whether it's gardening, painting, hiking, or playing an instrument, make time for these passions. They provide a necessary counterbalance to the demands of caregiving, refreshing your spirit and broadening your life experiences. This balance helps foster resilience, allowing you to return to your caregiving feeling more like yourself.

Incorporating these self-care strategies into your routine is essential, not optional. By taking care of your health, setting clear boundaries, taking regular breaks, and engaging in enjoyable activities, you are taking small yet continuous steps to provide better care for your loved one and your family.

Recognizing Signs of Caregiver Burnout and Acting

Burnout creeps in silently, often disguised as just another rough day, making it hard to recognize until you're deep under its weight. As a caregiver, you're constantly pouring from your emotional and physical reserves, and without realizing it, you might hit a point where you feel like you have nothing left to give. This state of emotional, physical, and mental exhaustion is what we refer to as caregiver burnout. It manifests in various ways, but here are some common symptoms (WebMD, 2022):

- Less interest in your hobbies and interests
- Less interest in spending time with friends and family
- Feeling hopeless or irritable
- Difficulty sleeping
- Changes in appetite or weight
- More bugs, illness, and viruses
- Emotional and/or physical exhaustion
- Turning to unhealthy coping strategies such as drinking or smoking

These signs are your body and mind's way of telling you that it's time to step back and take care of yourself. Once you acknowledge these feelings and signs, the next step is to seek help. This might mean talking to a professional therapist who can provide you with strategies to manage your stress and emotional turmoil. Therapy can be a safe space to express your feelings without fear of judgment, helping you process your emotions healthily. Opening up to trusted friends or family members about what you're experiencing can also provide relief. Sometimes, just voicing your struggles and knowing someone understands can lighten your emotional load significantly.

Creating a personal support plan is so beneficial. This plan involves identifying key individuals and resources that can support you when you're overwhelmed. Don't hesitate to ask for help. Often, the people around us are willing to help but might not know how. These could be friends who can provide a listening ear, family members who can step in and give you a break, or professional caregivers who can take over some of your responsibilities, even if just for a few hours each week. The idea is to have a ready list of resources to tap into when you feel you're nearing your limit instead of struggling until you pass your breaking point. This proactive approach helps manage stress and ensures that you have the support you need before reaching a breaking point.

Finally, it might help to change your approach to how you deal with your responsibilities. I know that I had a bad habit of focusing on everything that I needed to do rather than looking at how much I had achieved—and although my actions weren't perfect, I had done a fairly decent job. I decided that instead of berating myself for the laundry pile, I needed to take a moment to consider that I had done a good job cleaning in the short time I had. Then, I took the tasks that were left over (both daily and weekly) and turned them into goals. This enabled me to break down daunting tasks into smaller ones and reward myself for the progress I made. It was a successful strategy to turn the mundane into a little more fun.

Balancing Caregiving with Personal Life

For a caregiver, life includes both the tasks you need to fulfill for your loved one and personal activities, and using tools like planners and technology can help you make sure you are striking the right balance. Start by plotting out the fixed caregiving tasks, such as medication times or doctor's appointments. Then, around these fixed points, schedule your own essential and personal activities. It could be something as simple as a coffee break with a friend or time set aside for a hobby. Technology can greatly assist in this balancing act. Apps that allow you to set reminders or alarms can be a lifesaver, ensuring you don't lose track of time when you're absorbed in caregiving tasks. Also, consider digital calendars that can be shared with other family members or caregivers. This way, everyone is on the same page, and you can coordinate schedules so that everyone has the chance to find their balance.

It's easy to become isolated when your days are filled with the demands of caregiving. Friends and family are great for venting and supporting you, but don't forget that you need a break from care. I remember times when I would take a break from caring only to find myself spending the entire time talking about care anyway. Schedule time to release all your pent-up emotions, but then change the subject for a true break.

Setting realistic goals for yourself is both a grounding and a liberating practice. As a caregiver, you might feel pressured to meet high expectations in all areas of your life. However, it's important to acknowledge that not every day will be perfect, and not every task will be completed. Set goals that are achievable and allow some flexibility. This approach reduces the feeling of being overwhelmed and enhances your sense of accomplishment, keeping you motivated. Remember, your worth is not measured by how much you do each day but by the compassion and effort you bring to your numerous roles.

Managing your time, integrating help from your social circle, maintaining your external relationships, and setting achievable goals puts you on the right path to creating a balanced life. In many ways, it's nice to be needed and to show up for these people; just don't forget to show up for yourself as well.

Stress Management Techniques That Actually Work

If you want to prevent burnout, you need to manage stress levels. But it's more than just this; it's about cultivating a lifestyle that allows you to enjoy your caregiving role and maintain your well-being. Let's explore some effective ways to manage stress, which you can integrate effortlessly into your daily routine, even during those brief moments you catch between your caregiving tasks.

Effective Relaxation Techniques

One of the quickest and most effective ways to counteract the onset of stress is through relaxation techniques. Deep breathing exercises are a fantastic tool you can use anywhere, anytime, and are scientifically proven to work. Deep breathing activates the parasympathetic nervous system (the opposite of the fight or flight response) and sends signals to your body to calm down (The University of Toledo, n.d.). Try this: inhale slowly through your nose, allowing your chest and lower belly to rise as you fill your lungs. Let your abdomen expand fully. Then, exhale slowly through your mouth. Just a few rounds of this exercise can significantly calm your nervous system.

Another method is progressive muscle relaxation, which involves tensing each muscle group in your body intensely but briefly and then releasing. It's surprisingly effective at reducing physical tension and the psychological stress that often accompanies it (Cuncic, 2023). Guided imagery, where you visualize a peaceful setting or a desired outcome, can also redirect your mind away from stressors, providing a mental escape. Because the mind tends to wander, I use guided imagery videos online that offer prompts. Many videos incorporate deep breathing exercises, too.

Engaging in these practices regularly can help you manage stress before it escalates, keeping you centered and more prepared to face the challenges of caregiving. I know these sound too simple to be effective, but the secret to their effectiveness is consistency. I have had to use them many times over my years of being a caregiver, and I have noticed that I gain more from each one if I make them part of my daily routine instead of just using them in times of stress.

Adopting a Healthy Lifestyle

It may sound cliché, but a healthy diet, enough sleep, and regular exercise are essential for both managing stress and self-care. Eating a balanced diet provides the nutrients your body needs to function optimally and cope with stress. Foods rich in omega-3 fatty acids, like salmon, can decrease your stress levels, while a high-sugar and high-fat diet can do the opposite (Cleveland Clinic, n.d.). Sleep is just as important; it's your body's time to heal, regenerate, and process the emotional experiences of the day. Most adults need between seven to nine hours of sleep per night. If caregiving responsibilities are impinging on your sleep, consider strategies such as splitting night shifts with another family member or a professional caregiver. Finally, regular physical activity is an excellent stress reliever. Whether it's a brisk walk in the park or a thirty-minute workout session, exercise produces endorphins, which are chemicals in the brain that act as natural painkillers and mood elevators (Watson, 2024). These endorphins may also help relieve the physical aches and pains that come with looking after your loved one.

Cognitive Restructuring

Cognitive restructuring involves changing the negative thought patterns that can increase under stress. There is such a thing as negativity bias, a phenomenon where it's easier to believe the negative, and we pay more attention to negativity. Because our actions are often based on our thoughts, this negativity bias can play a significant role in our lives (Cherry, 2023). These thoughts tend to replay over and over in our heads until we are stuck in a cycle of negativity.

Start by observing your thoughts. Are they overly negative or critical? The biggest question to ask yourself is whether there is any evidence to support your thought (Concordia University, n.d.). Imagine telling yourself time and time again that you are a useless carer. Despite your negative thoughts, the evidence points to a loved one who is safe and is leading a life with the best quality possible for their situation. When you start to focus on the evidence and not on what the negativity bias leads you to think, you can restructure the original thought. "I'm a terrible carer" now becomes "I'm constantly learning and doing the best I can for my loved ones," a more positive and realistic thought. This technique reduces the stress caused by negative thought patterns while enhancing your problem-solving capabilities for challenging caregiving situations. It's about shifting your perspective to see the positives in your caregiving role, the strengths in your actions, and viewing challenges as opportunities for growth and learning.

Emergency Stress "STOP" Techniques

For those moments when stress feels overwhelming and you need to stop its escalation, the "STOP" technique can be a lifesaver. Here's how it works:

- **S**top what you are doing and take a step back.
- **T**ake a few deep breaths to help calm your mind and body.
- **O**bserve what's happening inside you. What are you thinking? How are you feeling?
- **P**roceed with an action that will support you in that moment. Maybe you need to delegate a task, take a break, or change your environment (Ferguson, 2022).

By applying this technique, you effectively interrupt the stress response and give yourself a chance to regroup and choose how best to move forward.

Incorporating these stress management techniques into your routine can change your feelings about caregiving. They empower you to handle stress more effectively, ensuring you remain a compassionate caregiver and a healthy, happy individual. Let's face it: Stress isn't going to just magically disappear, so it's crucial that you learn how to manage it so that the effects don't take such a toll on your well-being.

The Role of Mindfulness and Meditation in Caregiving

At its core, mindfulness involves being fully present, engaged, and aware of where we are and what we're doing, without being overly reactive or overwhelmed by what's happening around us (Headspace, n.d.). For caregivers, this practice can be a sanctuary, providing much-needed mental space in the daily challenges. It's not about emptying your mind of all thoughts, as that is just unrealistic. However, learning how to accept your thoughts and calm the mind can improve interactions with your loved ones and enhance your ability to cope with stress. Our minds are very valuable and deserve a break from the chaos.

Regular mindfulness and meditation practice have great benefits. Over time, they lead to improved mental clarity, making it easier to solve problems, make decisions, reduce anxiety, and build emotional resilience. Perhaps most importantly, mindfulness fosters a greater capacity for compassion for your loved one and yourself. Interestingly, research has also shown that mindfulness can improve memory and attention (Davis & Hayes, n.d.), two things that have definitely become a priority for me.

The basics of mindfulness start with understanding its principles: attention, intention, and attitude. Attention involves directing your focus to what is happening in the present moment, which could be as simple as noticing the sensations of your breathing or the sounds around you. This helps anchor you in the now, steering your mind away from worries about the future or regrets over the past. Intention refers to your reason for practicing mindfulness— perhaps to reduce stress or to be more present with your loved one. This intention sets the direction of your practice. Lastly, attitude involves the qualities you bring to mindfulness, such as curiosity, openness, and acceptance (Mindful Leader, n.d.). Approaching your experiences with these attitudes can significantly enhance your ability to manage caregiving's emotional ups and downs.

For those new to the practice, starting with simple meditation techniques can be incredibly beneficial. Mindfulness of breath is a fundamental technique where you focus on your breathing. Sit in a comfortable position, close your eyes, and observe the natural flow of your breath. Notice the air entering your nostrils, the rise and fall of your chest, or the sensation of air leaving your body. When your mind wanders, gently bring your attention back to your breath (Greater Good in Action, 2024).

This practice can be a calm port in the storm, helping you stay centered during the day's challenges. I can tell you that I didn't believe this would be helpful. I had never needed to incorporate anything like this in my life until I became my parent's caregiver. For me, it brought about a sense of peace, like that feeling you get when the sun is on your face. It's always a good idea to compare a "before and after" of how you feel when you try mindfulness so that you can see what sense of peace it brings you.

Another accessible practice is the body scan. This involves mentally scanning your body for areas of tension and consciously releasing it. Pay attention to each part of your body, starting from the top of your head and moving down to your toes (Raypole, 2022). This promotes relaxation and enhances bodily awareness, helping you tune in to the signals your body sends when it's becoming stressed or tired.

These practices can be done in just a few minutes, fitting easily into a busy caregiving schedule. As a nurse practicing Western medicine her entire career, this was very foreign to me. But I was willing to try anything when I was at the heaviest point of my parent's caregiving. My sister is a yoga instructor, so she helped me put these techniques into effect and really reap the benefits. If you struggle with any of these techniques, search for a short video online to use as a guide. Don't feel you need to try longer videos, as the short ones are enough to introduce you until you get confident.

Integrating mindfulness into your daily caregiving tasks can also transform how you experience these activities. Whether preparing meals, assisting with personal care, or managing medication, try to engage fully with the task. Notice the colors of the food, the feel of the water, or the sound of the pills rattling in the bottle. This focused attention helps reduce anxiety and increases your effectiveness and satisfaction in caregiving tasks. It turns routine activities into opportunities for mindfulness, allowing you to practice throughout the day without needing to carve out extra time. We all know that additional time is very scarce during caring.

Physical Health: Exercises and Activities for Caregivers

Regular physical exercise helps relieve the fatigue that often accompanies long hours of caregiving and boosts your mood and energy levels, enabling you to face each day with renewed vigor. I know it can feel impossible to muster up your last ounce of energy to start exercising, but it's worth it. It's about finding smart, flexible ways to incorporate physical activity into your day without it feeling like a burden.

Starting with something as simple as walking can make a noticeable difference. It doesn't require special equipment or a fitness studio—just comfortable shoes. Consider short walks around the neighborhood or a local park. These can provide you with some precious alone time, or you can bring your loved one with you, making it an enjoyable outing for both of you. The fresh air, change of scenery, and gentle physical activity can be incredibly rejuvenating. At-home workouts can be a godsend for days when getting out isn't possible. Numerous online platforms offer free or low-cost exercise videos ranging from yoga and Pilates to more vigorous aerobic workouts. These can be done in your living room in as little as ten to thirty minutes, fitting easily into a busy schedule.

Yoga, in particular, is a fantastic option for caregivers. It combines physical flexibility, strength, breathing exercises, and mindfulness, which can all help reduce stress. Even a few minutes of yoga can help center your thoughts and calm your mind, preparing you for the day ahead or helping you unwind after a challenging day. You can set up a small, dedicated space in your home where you can roll out a yoga mat, making sure this practice becomes a regular part of your routine.

Ergonomics plays an important role in caregiving, particularly in preventing the physical strain from lifting or assisting someone with mobility challenges. Learning proper lifting techniques is essential to avoid back injuries. For instance, bending your knees and keeping your back straight as you lift helps distribute weight more evenly and prevents strain. Additionally, ergonomic tools like adjustable beds, shower chairs, and specially designed transfer aids can make caregiving easier and safer for both of you. Investing in these tools promotes safety and helps conserve your energy throughout the day. I used these at work and when I was caring for my parents. We cannot afford to take the chance of injuring ourselves because our loved ones are so dependent on us.

Participation in group sports or fitness classes offers multiple benefits. These settings provide physical exercise and important social interaction. Local community centers often offer classes that cater to various interests and fitness levels, from dance classes to water aerobics. These classes can become something you look forward to, providing a fun and supportive environment where you can connect with others outside your world of caring and enjoy a break from your routine.

Incorporating regular physical activity into your life is not just about maintaining your health; it's about enriching your life and enhancing your ability to care for others. By choosing activities that fit your schedule and interests, you make exercise a much-anticipated part of your day rather than a chore. Whether it's a morning walk, a yoga session, or a weekly dance class, these physical activities provide vital energy, reduce stress, and foster a sense of well-being that permeates all aspects of your life. I did not commit to my physical health, and now I have an autoimmune disorder. I have paid the price for ignoring my health needs to give all I had to my parents. I am thankful I could do it, but it came at a cost. Caregiver stress and burnout are real. I always said I didn't have time to take care of myself when, really, it was only the guilt stopping me from finding the time... Please make the time for yourself!

As we close this chapter on caregiver health and well-being, remember that taking care of yourself is not an optional part of caregiving—it's essential. This comprehensive and holistic approach to self-care ensures that you can continue to provide the loving, effective care that your loved one depends on while living a fulfilling and balanced life yourself. As we move forward, the focus will shift to advanced caregiving topics, where we will explore deeper aspects of dementia care, ensuring you are equipped to handle the evolving challenges of this role.

Chapter 6

Advanced Caregiving Topics

I almost feel guilty talking about this matter because I know how hard it is to look at your loved one and know the inevitable will happen. Nevertheless, I also know that a lack of preparation can make advanced caregiving a living nightmare. Each step forward is uncertain, and the path often feels hidden and unpredictable. This part of your caregiving journey might bring more bewildering challenges, requiring deeper insights and more complex approaches. Here, we explore one of the most compassionate aspects of dementia care—palliative care—an approach that focuses on prolonging life and enhancing the remaining quality of life.

Palliative Care Approaches in Dementia

Palliative care is a specialized form of medical care designed to relieve the symptoms and stress of a serious illness. Its primary goal is to improve the patient's and family's quality of life. Unlike hospice care, which is typically reserved for the final months of life, palliative care can be provided alongside curative treatments. In dementia, where ongoing cognitive decline affects physical health, palliative care becomes an essential part of caregiving. It focuses on managing symptoms such as pain, confusion, and agitation and addresses psychological, social, and spiritual needs, providing a holistic approach to care. At the same time, palliative care is an excellent source of support for you, guiding you so that you know what to expect next (Hope Health, 2023).

Deciding when to integrate palliative care into your loved one's treatment plan can be a tough choice. It's often thought about too late in the disease progression, so it's important to recognize the indicators early. Significant decline in functional abilities, frequent hospitalizations due to complications from dementia, or a noticeable decrease in quality of life despite standard treatments are all signs that palliative care may be beneficial. Additionally, it might be time to consider this specialized support if managing daily care becomes overwhelming despite your best efforts and resources. Palliative care professionals can offer management strategies beyond the scope of routine dementia care, meaning it's far from a sign that you have failed.

Effective palliative care for dementia involves a variety of interventions tailored to meet the specific needs of the individual. Pain management, often overlooked in dementia patients who may have difficulty communicating discomfort, is a cornerstone of palliative care. Techniques can range from medication management to non-pharmacological methods such as massage, warm baths, or comfortable, non-restrictive clothing. Nutritional support is also crucial; as swallowing becomes challenging, a palliative care team might integrate specialized dietary plans or feeding techniques to ensure adequate nutrition.

Emotional and spiritual counseling forms another vital component of this care approach. Dementia can stir profound existential and spiritual questions for the patient and their family, and addressing these concerns can bring immense comfort. Palliative care teams often include chaplains or counselors who can navigate these sensitive areas, providing support tailored to the family's beliefs and values (Kinder Caring, 2024).

Working effectively with a palliative care team requires open communication and coordination. These professionals become an extension of your caregiving family, bringing their expertise to manage progressing symptoms and provide relief. It is important to share your insights about your loved one's preferences, previous lifestyle, and medical history to help the team effectively tailor their approach. Regular meetings with the palliative care team allow for ongoing adjustments according to your loved one's changing needs.

I want you to know that engaging with this team also means stepping into a partnership where your input as the primary caregiver is valued and necessary. It's a collaborative effort to enhance the well-being of someone you love, grounded in respect, compassion, and a shared goal of providing the best possible care. Don't feel like you will be left on the sidelines as someone else takes over.

Handling Severe Behavioral and Psychological Symptoms

There is no sugarcoating it! As this disease progresses, you might witness severe symptoms like psychosis, where your loved one might see or hear things that aren't there; aggression, which can manifest in shouting or even physical actions; and extreme agitation, where they seem perpetually restless or upset. These symptoms affect the well-being of your loved one and stretch your emotional and physical limits as a caregiver. Recognizing these behaviors as a part of dementia and not personal attacks can help you approach them with empathy and patience.

Psychosis in dementia might include hallucinations or delusions, which can be particularly distressing both for you and your loved one (Derrow 2020). Understanding that these experiences are very real to them is critical in managing your response. It's not about disproving their reality but gently guiding them to a safer mental space. Aggression, whether verbal or physical, often stems from frustration, confusion, or pain. It's a stark reminder of the importance of maintaining a safe environment where triggers are minimized. Extreme agitation can sometimes be the easiest to spot but the hardest to soothe, as it might stem from a mix of psychological discomfort and physical pain. If these episodes increase in frequency, duration, or intensity, you may need to lean on your palliative care team more.

At this point, medical interventions might be necessary, and this is where healthcare professionals' guidance becomes indispensable. Medications can be prescribed to help manage psychosis or reduce anxiety and aggressive behaviors. However, these should be approached with caution, always considering the potential side effects and the overall health of your loved one. Another friend of mine from a support group felt it was a case of deciding between the lesser of two evils. The aggressive behavior of his uncle had become too much for him to handle, and while the palliative care team was used to such behaviors, he felt that the benefits of antidepressants outweighed the potential risks of side effects.

The same can be said for antipsychotics, with some regulatory agencies warning of the increased risk of mortality in elderly patients (Marcinkowska et al., 2020). It's an excruciatingly difficult decision, so lean on the experts. Regular reviews with a geriatric psychiatrist or a neurologist who specializes in dementia care can ensure that any medications are effectively contributing to a higher quality of life for your loved one.

In situations where the individual's behavior might pose a risk to themselves or others, it's important to have strategies in place to de-escalate tension. This could mean having a designated safe room where they can go to calm down without feeling cornered. It's also vital to ensure that you, as the caregiver, know how to handle these situations physically. Training in non-confrontational techniques that can help guide your loved one away from harm or assist them in calming down without using force is important.

Again, engaging with your professional team is not a sign of failure on your part as a caregiver; rather, it's an acknowledgment of the complexity of dementia and the need for specialized knowledge in managing its symptoms. Handling severe behavioral and psychological symptoms of dementia is undeniably difficult. It tests your limits, demands your patience, and requires a deep well of compassion. But with the right strategies, a safe environment, and the support of medical professionals, you can provide care that manages these symptoms effectively and respects and honors the person you love so deeply.

Advanced Communication Strategies for Non-Responsive Patients

When your loved one can no longer communicate verbally, you need to drastically change how you connect with them. This shift often feels disheartening; words are our most familiar tools for sharing love, comfort, and care. Yet, in these moments, non-verbal communication becomes invaluable and can reveal its profound capacity to reach beyond spoken language, touching the heart and soul directly. Exploring non-verbal communication involves using touch, music, visual cues, and even the energy in your presence to convey what words cannot.

Touch, for instance, is a powerful communicator. A gentle hand squeeze, a warm hug, or the simple act of sitting closely can convey safety, love, and reassurance. When speaking to your loved one, maintaining physical contact can help keep them anchored, making your presence felt more deeply.

Sometimes I look back on some of the non-verbal moments I had with my parents and almost smile. At first, I used to try too hard to make conversation. I would ask my mom how she was, and she would smile and say, "Old!" and that was the end of the conversation. If I hadn't been around for lunch, I would ask what she had eaten, and she would just look at me as if I was talking in a foreign language. I learned that I was trying to force a conversation because I was afraid of the silence. Neither of my parents needed conversation; they just needed my presence, and it was fine if we sat in silence, listening to music or flicking through photo albums or magazines with pictures of hobbies they used to enjoy.

Documenting these non-verbal interactions is important for tracking progression and sharing with healthcare providers who can tailor their care approaches based on how your loved one responds. Keeping a detailed journal of what seems to engage or soothe them can guide the care team in enhancing therapeutic interventions, ensuring that these strategies evolve as your loved one's condition changes. This documentation acts as a bridge between your intimate understanding of your loved one and the medical insights provided by care professionals.

You'll find that communication is not lost but transformed in the quiet of non-verbal exchanges. It invites you to listen with your heart, to understand without words, and to connect in ways that transcend spoken language. Even though this transition can be tough, it offers chances for deep connection. It reminds us that love and understanding aren't just in our words but also in the silent moments waiting to be found.

Using Technology to Enhance Caregiving

I have always been technologically challenged. My kids were a tremendous asset in helping me learn and use new technology. Yet, as daunting as it may seem, integrating technology into your caregiving routine offers tools designed to simplify tasks, enhance safety, and maintain a connection with your loved one, even as traditional communication methods become challenging.

Consider the daily care tasks that fill your schedule—managing medications, ensuring safety, and engaging with your loved one. Advanced technological tools like automated medication dispensers are designed to relieve you from the constant worry of whether your loved one has taken their medication correctly and on time. These devices can dispense the right dose at the right time and alert you and your loved one when it's time to take their medication.

Smart home devices transform a regular home into a safer, more responsive environment. Imagine a home that adjusts lighting automatically to reduce the risk of falls or smart thermostats that maintain the perfect temperature to ensure comfort without constant monitoring. These devices can be controlled via smartphones or voice commands, making them easily accessible and allowing your loved one to retain control over their environment with simplicity and dignity.

Wearable health monitors take this a step further by monitoring health metrics such as heart rate, sleep patterns, and physical activity. This constant stream of data provides invaluable insights into your loved one's health and well-being, alerting you to potential issues before they become emergencies. For instance, a sudden change in physical activity or sleep patterns could indicate a need for medical attention, enabling you to act swiftly and proactively. You may also want to consider devices that connect directly to emergency services.

Communication technologies also play a pivotal role, especially as verbal communication becomes more challenging. Apps designed to facilitate communication through simplified interfaces can help you stay connected with your loved ones. These apps can convert text to speech, interpret touch into messages, and provide visual aids to help express feelings and needs.

Evaluating and choosing the right technology involves carefully considering the benefits and the potential challenges. When assessing a technology solution, consider how it fits into your existing care routines. Is it easy to use? Does it integrate well with other devices? Most importantly, does it enhance the comfort and well-being of your loved one without adding unnecessary complexity to their life? Seek out user-friendly technologies supported by reliable customer service so that help is on hand should you ever need it. Moreover, as much as possible, involve your loved one in the decision-making process. This ensures that the technology meets their needs and preferences and helps them feel in control of their care, which can encourage them to accept them and be more enthusiastic toward the technology.

As you navigate these options, remember that each tool you integrate into your caregiving routine is a bridge to a more manageable, fulfilling care experience that respects the dignity and independence of your loved one while never replacing the importance of the human connection.

Innovations in Dementia Care: What's on the Horizon?

As we stand on the brink of what may be revolutionary changes in dementia care, the pace of research and development is nothing short of awe-inspiring. Researchers around the globe are on a quest not only to understand dementia better but also to transform this understanding into practical applications that can radically improve the quality of life for those affected and not just dementia sufferers. Promising new treatments are currently in various trial stages, offering a beacon of hope where there was once resigned acceptance.

One of the most pivotal areas of research is the development of new drugs that go beyond symptom management to address the underlying causes of dementia. These include medications designed to reduce the buildup of amyloid plaques in the brain, a characteristic of Alzheimer's disease. Anti-amyloid medications lower the amount of beta-amyloid in the brain, which is what interrupts neurons communicating with each other. The Food and Drug Administration (FDA) has approved two anti-amyloid medications, donanemab (Kisunla) and lecanemab-irmb (Leqembi), though it's essential to understand that these are still early days. Both drugs have been shown to be effective in the early stages of Alzheimer's, but the benefit for more advanced Alzheimer's is still unknown. There may also be side effects like swelling of the brain, headaches, and dizziness, but again, it's early days, and these types of treatments are still promising (Langmaid, 2024).

Another exciting development is the use of immunotherapy to help the immune system identify and attack abnormal brain proteins, potentially slowing the progression of the disease. This new form of treatment could stimulate the immune system to activate microglia in the brain. Microglia destroy amyloid plaques directly, but in the Alzheimer's brain, they can't do their job properly (NIH, 2024).

In addition to pharmacological advances, significant strides are being made in diagnostic tools. Early detection of dementia is crucial for effective management, and new technologies are emerging that can diagnose dementia long before symptoms become apparent. Blood tests that can detect biomarkers associated with dementia are currently being refined, and advanced imaging techniques are being developed that can provide detailed brain scans, identifying changes that hint at the onset of dementia. Another test for biomarkers is the cerebrospinal fluid test done through a spinal tap. This test can detect changes in markers such as tau and beta-amyloid (Alzheimer's Association, n.d.-b).

Looking ahead, technology's potential to transform dementia care is immense. Artificial intelligence (AI) is at the forefront of this transformation, with researchers developing AI-driven diagnostics that can analyze medical data with astonishing accuracy and speed. Scientists at Cambridge University have developed a machine learning model that can predict whether mild symptoms will develop into Alzheimer's and even the speed at which symptoms may develop. Testing has shown this AI model to be around three times more accurate than the current standard of care (University of Cambridge, 2024). These systems can spot subtle patterns in data that humans might miss, leading to earlier and more accurate diagnoses.

Virtual reality (VR) is another area where exciting potential is unfolding. VR environments can be used to provide cognitive stimulation in a controlled setting, which can be particularly beneficial for individuals with dementia. VR can provide dementia patients with a realistic trip down memory lane so they can revisit their past meaningful experiences or even travel to places they never got the chance to (Applewood Our House, n.d.) These environments can be tailored to individual preferences and needs, providing mental stimulation and a temporary escape from the constraints of daily life.

Advanced biotechnologies are also set to play a crucial role in the future of dementia care. Gene editing techniques, such as CRISPR, hold the promise of not just treating but potentially preventing dementia (Bhardwaj et al., 2022). While this is still a long way from clinical application, the research is advancing rapidly, and its possibilities are a testament to the innovative spirit driving dementia care forward.

It is essential to address any ethical challenges presented by these advancements as we embrace them. The adoption of new technologies and treatments raises important questions about patient consent, particularly in the context of individuals whose cognitive abilities are impaired. Ensuring that patients and their families are fully informed about the benefits and risks of new treatments is essential.

Privacy issues are also at the forefront, especially with technologies that monitor or collect personal health data. Balancing the benefits of such technologies with the right to privacy requires careful consideration and vigorous safeguards to protect sensitive information.

Staying informed is essential for caregivers and patients in this rapidly changing landscape. Subscribing to medical journals focusing on neurology and geriatrics can provide updates on the latest research and treatment options. Joining specialist groups or associations related to dementia care can also offer valuable resources and networking opportunities, connecting you with experts and other caregivers who can share their insights and experiences.

Attending conferences, whether in person or virtually, is another excellent way to stay informed. These events provide information on the latest developments and offer workshops and seminars that can enhance your caregiving skills. They provide a platform for community building, where shared experiences and knowledge foster a supportive network that can guide you through the complexities of dementia care. It's perfectly normal if some of the technical jargon goes over your head. Don't be scared to take notes because they will help you to carry out your own research later. Regardless of your source of information, keeping up to date with technology and medicine will help you make the best decisions for your loved one and provide you with hope for the future.

Preparing for End-of-Life Care: A Compassionate Approach

Discussing end-of-life wishes with your loved one and their care team can be one of the most challenging conversations you'll ever engage in. This topic is emotional and delicate, and a kind and clear approach that balances empathy and understanding is needed. The goal here isn't just to outline the medical or logistical preferences for end-of-life care but to ensure that these discussions reflect the values, beliefs, and wishes of your loved one. Start these conversations early, when your loved one can still express their wishes clearly. Approach the topic with sensitivity, ensuring they understand that the purpose is to honor their choices and provide care that aligns with their desires.

Legal and ethical considerations play a critical role in these discussions. Advance directives and do-not-resuscitate (DNR) orders are very important tools that ensure your loved one's wishes are respected, even when they can no longer communicate those wishes themselves. A medical provider has to complete a DNR form, and they will be able to help you with things like a wallet card or a bracelet so that your loved one's wishes are clear to others, especially in the case of an emergency. Your loved ones' wishes should be included in their living will. Your loved one needs to be mentally capable to sign a DNR, and if they are mentally sound, they can change their mind (MedlinePlus, n.d.). If they aren't capable, a legal guardian or family member can make this decision, and this can be made easier if you have talked about their wishes in the past.

These documents should be prepared well in advance and revisited periodically to ensure they continue to reflect your loved one's preferences as their situation and desires evolve. The ethical dilemmas often arise when family members or medical professionals have differing opinions about the best course of action. It's essential to manage these situations by fostering open, honest dialogue among all parties involved, always centering the conversation around the known or expressed wishes of your loved one.

Creating a comforting environment for your loved one during their final days is about both physical comfort and nurturing the soul. Personalize their space with items that bring joy and peace, whether family photos, a favorite quilt, or a playlist of cherished songs. Soft lighting, familiar scents, and a quiet atmosphere can help create a serene setting where your loved one can feel relaxed and loved. Small gestures, like reading to them, playing their favorite music, or simply holding their hand, can significantly affect their comfort levels.

Support for caregivers is just as important. Watching a loved one approach the end of life is profoundly stressful and emotional. Recognizing when you need to step back and take time for your mental health is crucial. You may find grief counseling helpful if the emotional weight is overwhelming, and consider respite care services to give yourself a necessary break. Community support resources can also be invaluable during this time, providing practical help and emotional solidarity.

Remember that this time is about honoring their life and the love you share. It's about ensuring their comfort and dignity in their final days and supporting each other through the challenges of farewell. By approaching end-of-life care with compassion, clarity, and respect for your loved one's wishes, you create a legacy of love that endures beyond their passing.

This chapter on advanced caregiving topics closes with a reaffirmation of our deepest commitment—to care with compassion, respect individuality, and cherish every moment given. Even if the latest science seems daunting, technology, new medications, and professionals are so important for quality of life, and embracing them can make all the difference. As we turn the page to the next chapter, we carry forward the lessons learned, the strength gained, and the love deepened through this profound caregiving experience.

Chapter 7

Enhancing Quality of Life

The golden rays of the late afternoon sun often remind me of the precious moments I spent with my parents in their garden, even as dementia slowly altered our familiarity. In these quiet moments, I found a profound truth: even in the grip of dementia, there are countless opportunities to create joy and share beautiful moments. This chapter is dedicated to helping you discover and nurture these moments of joy with your loved one, transforming everyday interactions into treasures of happiness and connection.

Creating Joyful Moments: Activities to Engage Your Loved One

Enhancing the quality of life for a person with dementia lies in personalizing activities that resonate with their past interests while aligning with their current capabilities. It's about adapting to their world and finding ways to bring joy and engagement through meaningful and feasible activities. Let's explore how simple pleasures, interactive games, and celebrating small successes can enrich your loved one's daily life, bringing smiles and a sense of accomplishment.

Personalized Activities

Remembering who they were before dementia is key to connecting with who they are now. This might mean modifying activities they once loved to match their current skill level. For instance, if your loved one was an avid gardener, they might now enjoy helping you water plants, deadhead flowers, or sort seeds. It's about focusing on the process rather than the outcome, ensuring the activities are enjoyable and stress-free. Tailoring activities in this way sparks joy and helps maintain their identity and self-esteem, which are often eroded by the disease.

Simple Pleasures

Engaging in simple, everyday tasks can provide a profound sense of normalcy and achievement. Activities such as folding laundry, setting the table, or clipping coupons can be therapeutic. They provide a sense of purpose and involvement in daily life, which is crucial for emotional health. These tasks should be approached with encouragement and patience, allowing them to perform at their own pace and celebrating their participation more than precision.

Interactive Games and Puzzles

Games and puzzles are excellent for cognitive stimulation, but their greatest value in dementia care is the joy and interaction they facilitate. My parents loved card games and would play for hours if I kept an old country station on the radio. Opt for games and puzzles that are simple enough to avoid frustration but engaging enough to be meaningful. Customized jigsaw puzzles made from family photos can be particularly impactful, as they connect cognitive exercise with personal memories, making the activity both brain-stimulating and heartwarming. Similarly, card games that involve matching colors or suits can promote problem-solving skills and provide a fun way to interact with your loved one, fostering connection and laughter.

Celebrating Small Successes

In dementia care, every small success is worth celebrating. These celebrations can significantly enhance your loved one's sense of accomplishment and self-worth. Did they complete a puzzle? Share a high-five. Managed to remember a recent event? Express genuine delight—with a huge emphasis on genuineness, as there is no need to insult their intelligence. These celebrations do more than acknowledge their efforts; they reinforce positive behavior and boost their morale. Moreover, sharing these successes with family members through stories or photos can help maintain a sense of community and support, reminding everyone involved in the care process of the joyful moments amidst the challenges.

As you integrate these strategies, observe which activities bring the most smiles and engagement, and make them regular features in your schedule. This personalized, joy-focused approach is what truly transforms the caregiving experience, bringing light and laughter into the days of those we love, even as they navigate the complexities of dementia.

Bringing Comfort and Fun into Your Loved One's Home

Let's briefly go back to the alternative therapies we have covered because you don't need a qualified professional to reap the rewards. Music therapy can be as simple as tuning in to the individual's favorite radio station or creating a playlist of their favorite songs from young adulthood, tunes from their wedding, or lullabies they sang to their children. If you know someone with instruments, consider borrowing a few and encourage your loved one just to play around. Simple instruments like tambourines, maracas, or homemade instruments can make this interaction fun and engaging. The goal isn't to create a musical masterpiece; it's a chance for you to see them enjoy themselves and create a precious memory for you to hold on to. Sing-alongs are another fantastic way to engage family members of all ages. If your loved one can, dancing can add a physical element to the musical experience, providing gentle exercise and a lot of laughs.

After looking at the benefits of pet therapy, you might be tempted to get a new pet for your loved one. Of course, there is nothing wrong with this, but careful consideration is needed. It's important to assess the individual's ability to interact safely with a pet, their comfort and experience with animals, and their ability to understand and respect an animal's boundaries. The type of pet is also important to consider. Dogs and cats are common choices, but the breed's temperament should match the person's needs. For instance, a calm, older dog might be better suited than a high-energy puppy for someone with dementia. Additionally, hypoallergenic breeds might be necessary if allergies are a concern.

You also need to be realistic about taking on a new pet as it's likely that a lot of the responsibility. Breaking away from the traditional pets, you may want to consider fish or rabbits that are lower maintenance. I once visited a care home with an aquarium where many residents would sit around watching the different breeds of fish for hours. Despite wanting the best for your loved one, you can't ignore the fact that pets become an integrated part of the family and also must have their needs met. For this reason, you may also want to consider organizations that offer temporary foster services or short-term care.

Finally, there is art therapy. Much like music therapy, there is no need to set intentions to create a masterpiece. What's wrong with taking some paints and just flicking colors onto a canvas or blending colors with finger paints? All you need is a box of materials with different media, such as paints, pencils, chalk, or pens. I once bought some fabric markers and made t-shirts with my children and my parents.

Whether it's a pet or a pot of paint, accept the fact that things might get messy. I loved to remind myself that if it's too perfect, it's not real, and right now, real is what matters.

Adapting Hobbies to Suit Cognitive Decline

Imagine not being able to do your favorite hobby ever again. As if it's not enough that you have a chronic and progressive disease, soon the things you loved doing will no longer be possible. Look at it from your loved one's perspective, and it's easy to see how mental health can quickly decline. While it's true some hobbies may not be appropriate, it's also essential that we learn how to modify others to maintain engagement and happiness.

The first step in this adaptation process is assessing their current cognitive and physical abilities. This isn't about focusing on their lost skills but rather about celebrating and utilizing what they can still do and enjoy. Observing how they manage daily tasks can give clues about their fine motor skills, problem-solving abilities, and attention span. For example, audiobooks could be an excellent alternative if they can still enjoy stories but struggle to read.

The key to modifying their favorite activities is to simplify them to reduce frustration while still providing a sense of achievement and enjoyment. Take painting, for instance. If your loved one was a painter but now finds detailed work challenging, switch to larger canvases with bigger brushes, or try finger painting, which can be wonderfully tactile and liberating. Similarly, if they enjoy gardening, consider raised planters or container gardening, which can be easier to manage and less physically demanding. The goal is to adjust the activity to their current ability level so they can engage without feeling overwhelmed.

Introducing new hobbies can also be a refreshing way to stimulate their interest and engagement. The trick is to introduce new activities slowly and gauge their reaction. Start with hobbies that require minimal learning or new skills. Simple crafting projects like making collages from old magazines or assembling bead jewelry are good for fine motor skills and a sense of accomplishment. Digital photography, especially with a simple point-and-shoot camera, can be a great hobby, too. It allows them to capture moments from their daily life, which can later serve as conversation starters and memory aids.

Active engagement and interaction during these activities are fundamental. They keep your loved one mentally and physically involved and provide essential emotional connections. Your role during these activities is to be present. You're not there as a teacher or supervisor who has to tell them what to do. Celebrate their efforts, focus on the pleasure of the activity itself rather than the outcome, and always be ready to adjust the task to ensure it remains within their comfort zone. This approach helps boost their self-esteem while you both have quality time together.

Celebrating Milestones and Creating New Traditions

It's easy to think that because someone may not remember specific events, they don't find joy in celebrating them. However, emotional memory—the feelings of love, happiness, and security —often remains intact for far longer than specific memories. Celebrating birthdays, anniversaries, or other significant dates can bring a sense of normalcy and festivity vital for the person with dementia and their family. It's not about the date itself but the celebration and the positive emotions it can evoke. For instance, a simple birthday party with a favorite cake and a few close family members can be extremely meaningful, providing feelings of love and belonging.

Creating new traditions can also be a wonderful way to adapt to the evolving capabilities of your loved one with dementia while still making every day special. These traditions can be simple, like a weekly family dinner or an evening walk around the neighborhood. What's important is the regularity and the sense of expectation it creates. These traditions become rituals your loved one can look forward to, providing anchor points that help maintain a sense of time and continuity. For example, if your loved one has a passion for the ocean, a weekly trip to the beach can help them connect with their past interests.

Documenting these special moments is significant, not just for reminiscence but also for connection. In a digital age, capturing memories through photos or videos has never been easier. Creating a digital album or a printed photo book of celebrations and daily joys can provide a valuable tool for reminiscence therapy, which is known to help improve mood and cognitive function (Cammisuli et al., 2022). Sharing these albums with visitors or caregivers who may not be family can help them connect better with your loved one, providing context and sparking conversations that might otherwise be difficult to initiate.

Inclusive planning ensures that any celebration or new tradition considers your loved one's preferences and comfort. This means choosing not to overwhelm environments, keeping guest lists small, and maintaining a familiar and calm setting. It's also important to be mindful of timing, as planning an activity when you know they are prone to sundowning can lead to adverse results. Additionally, involving them in the planning process as much as possible can provide a sense of control and participation. Simple decisions, like choosing things for the menu, can make activities more engaging and meaningful.

Embracing these practices of celebrating milestones, creating new traditions, and documenting memories will strengthen family bonds and create enduring memories for everyone involved. As you integrate these elements into your caregiving, they become more than just activities—they evolve into cherished moments highlighting the enduring power of love and family, even in the face of dementia.

Environmental Modifications for a Happier Home

An environment that reduces confusion and promotes peace can have a tremendously positive impact on your loved one's mood and behavior. Let's explore ways to create such an environment, focusing on soothing aesthetics, sensory-friendly modifications, and personal touches that echo their life story and preferences.

The ambiance of a home can influence anyone's mood, and this is especially true for someone with dementia whose ability to process sensory input is altered. With dementia, you might find a person struggles with depth perception, might lose tactile sensation, or might have problems filtering out background noise. It's also possible that they are startled more easily (Kohlbrenner, 2022). Although we have covered the safety aspect of home modification, there are still some sensory changes that can further help. Soothing colors in your home decor can have a calming effect; soft blues, greens, and warm, neutral tones can soothe anxiety and agitation. Consider repainting walls or incorporating these colors through curtains, bedding, and upholstery.

Creating areas in your home that cater to sensory sensitivities can significantly enhance comfort. For instance, create a quiet corner with a comfortable chair, a soft throw blanket, and perhaps a small indoor fountain to provide gentle, soothing sounds. This can be a sanctuary where your loved one can retreat when feeling overwhelmed. Textures are also important; incorporating elements like a plush rug or soft pillows can provide tactile comfort and reduce anxiety.

Personalizing the living space of someone with dementia is about more than aesthetics; it's about connection. Decorate their environment with items that speak to their life's story. Hang family photographs at eye level where they can see them often, or display mementos that carry personal significance, such as awards, handmade crafts from grandchildren, or souvenirs from favorite trips. These personal touches beautify the space and serve as cognitive aids.

Transforming a living space into a sanctuary that supports the well-being of someone with dementia creates a calming environment with sensory-friendly spaces so that safety is infused with personal elements. As you implement these modifications, observe how they positively affect your loved one and continue to adjust as needed to meet their evolving preferences and needs. You might not get it right the first time, so don't worry. I remember taking a while to fiddle with the lights and air conditioning until I was able to get the right settings for both parents. Keep your calm, and know that every adjustment you make is giving your loved one a better quality of life.

We've explored a range of strategies and modifications to make your home a more dementia-friendly place. These adjustments are vital in creating a supportive environment that increases comfort and, at the same time, enhances the quality of life for your loved one. I have my fingers crossed that you will never need this final chapter, but at the same time, it's full of information I wish I had had because my parents and I had to face a few crises. Try not to skim over these remaining sections, as having this knowledge under your belt makes you prepared for everything!

Chapter 8

Navigating Challenges and Crisis Management

Imagine you're enjoying a quiet afternoon, and your loved one with dementia is peacefully reading a magazine next to you. Suddenly, the power goes out, or a massive storm scares them, leading to confusion and agitation. As much as we try to cultivate a calm and controlled environment, emergencies can and do happen. How prepared are we? The truth is that the unpredictable nature of emergencies can be particularly challenging when caring for someone with dementia. But with thoughtful preparation and strategies, you can handle these tough times with confidence and keep your loved one as calm as possible.

Emergency Preparedness for Dementia Caregivers

The key to being ready for emergencies is having a thorough plan. This plan serves as your guide during unexpected events and should include necessary contact information, medical information about your loved one, and clear escape routes from your home. Start by listing all emergency contacts—doctors, family members, close friends, and local emergency services. Include their phone numbers, addresses, and email addresses. Next, compile a detailed medical profile for your loved one, which includes their current medications, dosages, allergies, and any specific medical instructions that could be critical in an emergency.

Mapping out escape routes is equally important. Walk through your home and identify the safest and most accessible exits. If you live in a multi-story building, consider the needs of your loved one and how quickly you can evacuate if the elevators are out of service. Also, if you have any questions about the best procedure, you can contact the local Red Cross or emergency management agency for advice (Administration for Community Living & National Alzheimer's and Dementia Resource Center, n.d.). Place these plans in several accessible locations and ensure every family member and regular visitor knows and understands where they are. It's also wise to practice evacuation drills regularly, adapting them as the cognitive and physical abilities of your loved one change. This practice keeps the plan fresh in everyone's minds and helps calm anxiety by providing a sense of preparedness.

In addition to a solid plan, having an emergency kit tailored to the specific needs of someone with dementia can be a game-changer. Consider the following items for your emergency kit.

- At least a week's supply of all medications, clearly labeled
- A medication schedule
- Copies of important documents like identification, health insurance information, and legal documents, such as power of attorney or advance directives
- Several sets of spare clothes

- Their favorite snacks
- Comfort items such as a favorite blanket, sweater, or photos

Keep this kit in a designated, easily accessible spot and check its contents regularly to replace expired medications and update documents as needed.

Effective communication during an emergency is key to ensuring the safety and well-being of your loved one. Educate yourself on how to quickly and accurately convey your loved one's condition and needs to emergency responders. Use simple and direct language. Despite my attempts to stay calm in my family's emergency, I found it hard to remain composed and found myself waffling and barely making sense. In the end, I had a written statement prepared that detailed the most critical information about my parents' dementia and typical behavior patterns. This can prevent misunderstandings and ensure that your loved one receives appropriate care and consideration from professionals who may be unfamiliar with their history.

Managing emergencies requires foresight, calm, and a well-established plan. Invest time in creating detailed emergency strategies and practice them regularly so you are ready for unexpected situations. This preparedness safeguards the physical health of your loved one, and it also provides peace of mind so you can handle crises with competence and care.

Dealing with Hospitalizations and Medical Emergencies

Hospital visits can be unsettling for anyone, but for a loved one with dementia, they can feel like a bewildering disruption to their familiar world. Preparing for these visits involves more than just having a bag packed. It means setting the stage for as smooth an experience as possible for you and your loved one. It's highly likely that your loved one gets distressed in a hospital, and a little perspective can help you see why. First, there is the unfamiliarity and the break from their comforting routine. Then, you have to consider the sensory aspect of a hospital. There are crowds, bright lights, and often loud noises. I feel overwhelmed in hospitals, so I struggle to imagine what this sensory overload must do to someone with dementia.

Many of the items in your emergency kit are needed for a hospital kit, too, such as spare clothes, a favorite blanket, or a photo of family members for comfort. Don't assume that just because it's a hospital, they will have a complete medical history of your loved one. It's always best to be safe rather than sorry and take all the medical documentation you have. These documents can be invaluable in ensuring that medical staff have a clear understanding of your loved one's health background without wasting time having to consult with various specialists.

Communication with hospital staff is crucial and can greatly impact the care your loved one receives. Always advocate clearly and calmly for your loved one's needs. It's helpful to explain how dementia affects their communication and behavior, particularly under stress or discomfort. For example, it's incredibly helpful to let medical staff know if your loved ones tend to forget to drink or if a certain smell agitates them. Clarifying these nuances can guide the staff in their approach, making the experience less stressful for everyone involved. Additionally, try to maintain as much consistency as possible during the hospital stay. If there are routines that are particularly soothing or stabilizing, discuss with the nursing staff how these might be integrated into their daily care plan.

Familiarize yourself with the patient rights and advocacy services available in the hospital to make your experience less daunting. Understanding these can empower you to better advocate for your loved one's needs and rights. For instance, if a particular treatment plan seems more disorienting or distressing for your loved one, knowing their rights can help you discuss alternatives more effectively with the healthcare team. Don't hesitate to ask questions about any procedures or policies that aren't clear to you. Hospital staff are there to help, and clarifying these elements can help you feel more in control and assured.

Managing stress during hospital stays is as much about looking after yourself as caring for your loved one. Hospital environments can be intense, and watching a loved one in distress is never easy. Make sure you take breaks, step outside for fresh air, or grab a coffee. Managing your stress levels is vital, so don't forget to make the most of the techniques we covered previously. Consider alternate shifts with other family members or friends so you can rest knowing your loved one is not alone. It only takes small steps to help maintain your resilience, enabling you to be the rock your loved one relies on during such chaotic times.

Transitioning back home after a hospital stay involves careful preparation to ensure that your loved one's return is as comfortable and safe as possible. Before discharge, discuss with the care team any changes in care needs and any new medications or treatments that have been prescribed. This discussion should also cover any necessary modifications to your home environment to accommodate new mobility or care needs. Additionally, follow-up care, whether with home health services or outpatient therapies, should be arranged to ensure continuity of care and peace of mind as you adjust to being back home.

When to Consider a Higher Level of Care

Caring for someone with dementia at home is a profound expression of love and commitment. However, there may come a time when the care needed surpasses what can be provided in the home environment. Recognizing this point is necessary, not just for the well-being of your loved one but also for your own health. It's not about giving up or abandoning them.

Signs that might indicate a need for a higher level of care include increasing medical needs that require professional monitoring, a decline in the ability to perform daily activities, or significant changes in behavior that pose safety risks. I remember one person's mother-in-law kept having TIAs (transient ischemic attacks) or "mini-strokes" as a symptom of her vascular dementia (Stroke Association, n.d.), and when he found her on the kitchen floor one day, he knew it was time for the further care that the family couldn't provide. Additionally, if you find your own health deteriorating due to the stress and demands of caregiving, it might be time to consider additional help.

There is a full spectrum of care options available, from assisted living facilities that offer some level of independence to specialized dementia care units that provide intensive support. Each option has its own benefits and considerations. Assisted living might be suitable for those in the earlier stages of dementia who need minor assistance with daily activities but still enjoy a level of independence. On the other hand, nursing homes or specialized dementia care facilities might be more appropriate for those in the advanced stages of dementia who require twenty-four-hour care. Evaluating these options involves considering the current needs of your loved one, visiting various facilities, speaking with care staff, and discussing care philosophies to ensure they align with your loved one's needs and your family's values. It's also a good idea to look for facilities that cater to both assisted living and dementia units. This way, when the disease progresses, they can be moved to the next level of care within the same complex rather than being moved to a completely new location, which can be extremely disorientating.

Deciding to transition a loved one to a care facility is profoundly difficult and often accompanied by feelings of guilt and grief. It's natural to feel like you're letting your loved one down or not fulfilling a promise to keep them at home. However, it's important to reframe this decision as a step toward ensuring they receive the best care possible—a decision made from love and the desire to do what's best for them. Allow yourself to grieve the loss of this phase of caregiving, but also recognize that you are making a responsible choice in the interest of their safety and quality of life.

Making the transition as smooth as possible involves thoughtful preparation and attention to detail. Start by personalizing their new space with familiar items from home, such as photos, blankets, or a favorite chair. These items can make the new environment feel more comforting and less foreign. Maintaining regular visits, especially during the initial transition period, is also important to help your loved one adjust and feel supported. Engage with the care staff and establish a communication routine to keep updated on your loved one's adjustment and any changes in their care plan.

My parents had many other health issues that offered daily challenges. Planning ahead for sudden hospitalizations helped all of us handle the situation better. Unfortunately, as the disease progressed, we had to admit that it was too much, and we needed more help. Placing my parents in a care facility was the hardest thing I ever had to do. My dad's dementia progressed so quickly that he was moved into an acute setting and passed within months. My mom passed away exactly four months later... we believe from a broken heart. I live with that every day, but at the same time, I also know that the decision I made, albeit the hardest one of my life, was ultimately the best thing I could have done for them.

Navigating the decision and process of transitioning to a higher level of care is an act of courage and an expression of deep commitment to the welfare of your loved one. It underscores the dynamic nature of dementia caregiving, where sometimes love means making tough decisions that lead to the best care and quality of life for those we hold dear. As you move forward, I would like to remind you that seeking the best possible care environment is a continuation of your commitment, not an end to it.

Coping with the Loss of a Loved One

When you care deeply for someone with dementia, the slow nature of the decline may mean you begin grieving long before they pass away. This anticipatory grief is a complex mix of emotions—sadness, loss, and sometimes relief—that caregivers experience as they watch their loved ones gradually fade away. You may find yourself feeling numb, fearful, and even angry at the person for dying (Healthdirect, n.d.). It goes beyond mourning the inevitable loss of life; it's about grieving the loss of the person's memories and the shared moments that dementia strips away. Recognizing this form of grief is significant because it allows you to understand that these feelings are normal and not a sign of giving up on your loved one.

Managing anticipatory grief involves acknowledging your emotions and giving yourself permission to feel them fully. It's okay to be sad about your loved one's decline, to feel angry about the situation, or even relieved at moments when the burden eases slightly. These feelings do not mean you care any less. Sometimes, writing down your thoughts and feelings in a journal can help you process these complex emotions. It creates a private, unfiltered space where you can express yourself freely and reflect on your experiences without judgment. Talking about these feelings with trusted friends, family members, support groups, or a therapist can provide the support you need. They can offer consolation and different perspectives that might help you cope more effectively.

When the time comes and your loved one passes away, the grief doesn't end—it evolves. While you might feel prepared due to the anticipatory grieving, the finality of death brings its own intense emotions. It's important to continue to lean on your support system during this time. Stay connected with those who understand and can provide the emotional backing you need. Participating in memorial activities can also be a therapeutic way to channel your grief. Celebrating the life of your loved one can take many forms, such as organizing a memory walk in their honor, planting a garden, or compiling a photo album or digital slideshow of happy memories. These acts of remembrance honor your loved one and help you and others to remember the person beyond their illness, keeping the joy and love they brought into the world alive.

Self-care is incredibly important during this time. Grieving can be exhausting, both emotionally and physically. Make sure to give yourself space to rest and heal. Maintaining a routine that includes time for activities you enjoy, eating well, and getting enough sleep can help you through the grieving process. Sometimes, seeking professional help is necessary to navigate this challenging time. Therapists can provide strategies to cope with grief, helping you understand your emotions and find ways to move forward.

Allowing yourself to find a new normal after the loss of a loved one is a gradual process. It involves accepting that life has changed and finding ways to adapt without the physical presence of the person you cared for. This might mean redefining your daily routines, finding new hobbies, or even volunteering in areas supporting dementia awareness or caregiving. These steps do not mean you are forgetting your loved one; rather, they signify that you are learning to live a life that honors their memory while also caring for your well-being.

Remember that grief is a deeply personal experience and that there is no "right" way to work through it. Everyone finds different paths to healing, and all emotions you feel along the way are valid. Of course, people are going to want to offer you words of comfort and advice from their own experiences, but you are best trusting your instincts and listening to what your body is telling you.

Advocacy and Rights for Dementia Patients

When caring for a loved one with dementia, understanding and advocating for their rights is not just a responsibility—it's a fundamental aspect of providing compassionate and effective care. Dementia patients have the same rights as anyone else to dignity, privacy, and appropriate medical care, yet the nature of their condition often jeopardizes these rights. It's crucial that you, as a caregiver, are well-equipped to stand up for these rights. This means being both a shield and a spokesperson, making sure their right to quality care and respect is upheld in every setting, from home to the doctor's office.

The first step in effective advocacy is understanding the rights of your loved one. I highly recommend reading the full set of dementia statements, but here is a summary of them:

- **We have the right to be recognized as who we are.** A diagnosis isn't what should define your loved one.
- **We have the right to continue with day-to-day family life.** Dementia patients shouldn't be discriminated against or be subject to loneliness or unfair costs.
- **We have the right to an early and accurate diagnosis.** This includes appropriate and compassionate treatment from qualified professionals.
- **We have the right to be respected and recognized as partners in care.** Patients should be part of their care plan and decisions about the future.
- **We have the right to know about and decide if we want to be involved in research.** It shouldn't be assumed that anyone wants to be involved with research into the cause or cure (Alzheimer's Society, n.d.).

To actively advocate for these rights, developing effective communication techniques is essential. Clarity and assertiveness are key when interacting with healthcare providers or legal representatives. Prepare for meetings by writing down important points and questions in advance. This helps you remember critical details and shows that you are informed and committed to your loved one's care. Always express yourself clearly and calmly without being confrontational. It's about striking a balance between assertiveness and cooperation. Remember, you are there to build relationships that will benefit your loved one's care, not to create conflicts.

The legal systems protecting these rights can be intimidating, but understanding key elements can make a significant difference. For example, knowing how to set up or contest a power of attorney or guardianship could be fundamental to your loved one's care. These legal tools can help you make decisions on behalf of your loved one when they no longer can, ensuring their interests are protected. It's advisable to consult with a legal expert who specializes in elder law to guide you through this process. They can provide valuable insights and help you avoid common pitfalls.

Additionally, consider reaching out to local advocacy groups. These groups can offer specific advice on local laws and resources to aid your advocacy efforts. They often conduct workshops and seminars to enhance your understanding. Being well-informed empowers you to stand up for your loved one's rights and sets a foundation for providing the highest quality of care.

In essence, being an effective advocate means being informed, prepared, and willing to speak up for your loved one's rights. It involves a mix of understanding, patience, and assertiveness. By taking on this role with dedication and compassion, your loved one with dementia can be treated with the respect and dignity they deserve.

Reflecting and Planning for Future Caregiving Needs

Foresight is essential for the well-being of your loved one and for your peace of mind. Long-term care planning is more than just a practical necessity; it's a way to ensure continuity and quality of care as needs evolve. Engage in discussions about financial planning, care facility options, and even end-of-life care now so that you can approach these conversations thoughtfully and without the pressure of immediate decisions. When the time comes that your loved ones can't make their own decisions, you will be grateful for these insights to help you guide your decisions. It's about preserving the voice of your loved one at a time when they can express their wishes clearly. By setting a plan, you're paving a smoother road for you and your loved one.

I think evaluating your role as a caregiver is important. It's a role that will likely evolve as the demands of caregiving intensify. Assess your capacity realistically—consider your health, emotional resilience, and external responsibilities. It might be challenging to acknowledge, but there comes a time when professional care becomes necessary, not due to a lack of love or commitment but because the caregiving burden is too heavy to carry alone. Recognizing and acting on these limitations is a sign of strength and can lead to more sustainable caregiving arrangements.

Future-proofing your caregiving arrangements involves building a flexible system that can adapt to unforeseen changes. This might involve training other family members to handle specific caregiving tasks or setting up legal and financial structures to support long-term care needs. It also means staying informed about advancements in dementia care, which can offer new strategies and technologies that ease your caregiving responsibilities.

In reflecting on and planning for future caregiving needs, you're taking proactive steps to manage the evolving challenges of dementia care. Your comprehensive plan with care preferences and the evaluation of your caregiving tools can transform the caregiving experience for your loved one, yourself, and other family members. Dementia shouldn't just be about the fear of memory loss and reduced abilities. It should be about love, respect, and commitment to quality care, and you are now beyond capable of this.

Want to help other caregivers boost their capacity to care for loved ones?

Congratulations on completing your reading journey through this book. We have experienced many highs and lows and have seen how caring for a loved one with dementia involves creating joyful moments in the present while also preparing for future caregiving needs. If you once felt confused by the array of caregiving decisions you are constantly being called upon to make, I hope that this book has cleared away your doubts.

My aim was to provide you with a complete guide to the theoretical and practical knowledge you need to make your and your loved one's process a little lighter. When you have a plan in mind and you take the steps you need to set it in motion, it is much easier to cope with the inevitable challenges and surprises that come with caregiving. If this book has made your journey a little lighter, please let others know what you think.

TAKE A MOMENT TO SHARE YOUR THOUGHTS!

Thank you for reading this book. I wish you and your loved one many of the unique moments of connection that make caregiving such a profoundly rewarding experience.

Conclusion

As we draw the curtains on this journey through the pages of *Dementia Caregiving 101,* I want to take a moment to reflect on the path we've traveled together. Dementia caregiving is a journey marked by challenges, but it's crucial not to let these times overlook the profound moments of connection and deep personal growth. If you're feeling a mix of exhaustion and empowerment, know that you're not alone.

My mind is full of stories about my caregiving journey as a nurse and for my parents, but if I could pass on my most important lesson, it would be that caregiving is a delicate balance between taking care of the needs of your loved one and your own needs.

Starting with your loved one, the diagnosis process is going to be emotional, but the earlier, the better, so that you can take advantage of the latest advances in dementia. The next step is to start making necessary adjustments, and although we have discussed handrails and GPS systems, not all of this has to be done immediately. Taking away your loved ones' financial independence and adding additional locks to doors and windows can take away their dignity, which is something we want to maintain as much as possible. Instead of going over the top with safety measures that aren't necessary yet, use this time to get to know your loved one's wishes and, above all, spend quality time with them.

These early stages of the disease are also essential for organizing legal documents before your loved one loses the capacity to make decisions that impact their health, wishes, and finances. There is no fixed timeline for dementia. You may find there are months without significant changes, and then suddenly, symptoms progress at an alarming rate. This is why you need to prioritize matters that may only lead to more complications later.

In caregiving, as in life, there's no one-size-fits-all solution. Each person with dementia is a unique individual, and the care we provide must honor their individuality and dignity. It's about more than just meeting physical needs—it's about nurturing the soul, honoring past legacies, and cherishing each moment of connection. Whether it's music, arts and crafts, or gentle exercise together, every activity can be tailored to be rewarding, engaging, and beneficial for mental and physical well-being while making new memories for you to cherish.

It's also necessary to remember that caring for someone with dementia is a marathon, not a sprint. Your well-being is just as important as that of your loved one. I urge you to care for yourself with the same compassion and dedication you give freely to others. Focus on the three main elements of self-care: nutrition, exercise, and sleep. After this, you can plan activities that you enjoy and replenish your batteries. This isn't selfish and nothing you should feel guilty about. Please lean on your support network and seek professional advice when necessary. Time with people who understand some of what you are going through is time for you to vent and let out all those pent-up emotions, but don't forget to not allow dementia to be your only topic of conversation. Dementia shouldn't define your loved one, just as being a carer shouldn't define you. Don't hesitate to step back and recharge when needed.

The field of dementia is advancing, and with each new development, we can refine our approach to provide even better care. But beyond strategies and knowledge, remember the power of community. Let's advocate together for a society that supports and understands the needs of both those living with dementia and their caregivers. The burden is lighter when shared, and every small act of understanding and support can ripple out meaningfully.

I invite you, my fellow caregivers, to keep the conversation going. Share your stories, your challenges, and your victories. Join support groups, participate in online forums, or attend local events. Your experiences are invaluable, and your insights can light the way for others just starting on this path. There is another way that you can make your words count and have a positive impact on other caregivers' lives. A short review on Amazon can show other caregivers that there is an empathetic and practical guide that can support them in their journey. Every step toward dementia awareness can benefit us all. I thank you in advance, and I can't wait to hear your stories.

As you move forward, please take with you my deepest admiration and respect. Caregiving is not just a role but a testament to the human capacity for love and resilience. You are the unsung heroes in the lives of those you care for, and your journey

resonates with a profound and inspiring beauty. Here's to you—
the heart and soul of dementia caregiving.

My parents have been gone for three years now, and it still feels
like yesterday. It's possible that it has taken me this long to start
healing, and with all my heart, I hope this is different for you. I
also hope that this book can empower you to reach out. Find all
the help you can for your loved one and yourself. There is so much
more awareness of this disease and the needs of patients and
caregivers as well. Please don't do this alone. God bless.

References

Administration for Community Living & National Alzheimer''s and Dementia Resource Center. (n.d.). Emergency preparedness toolkit for people living with dementia. In *Unknown*. https://pblob1storage.blob.core.windows.net/public/nadrc/docs/2022-NADRC-Emergency-Prep-Toolkit-04202022.pdf

Alzheimer's Association. (2023, March 20). Self-care for caregivers: six science-backed tips that''ll help support you. *Alzheimer's and Dementia Blog - Alzheimer's Association of Northern California and Northern Nevada -*. https://www.alzheimersblog.org/2023/03/20/self-care-for-caregivers-six-science-backed-tips-thatll-help-support-you/

Alzheimer's Association. (n.d.-a). *Legal planning*. ALZ. https://www.alz.org/help-support/i-have-alz/plan-for-your-future/legal_planning

Alzheimer's Association. (n.d.-b). *Medical tests for diagnosing Alzheimer''s*. https://www.alz.org/alzheimers-dementia/diagnosis/medical_tests#:.

Alzheimer's Association. (n.d.-c). *Vascular dementia*. ALZ. https://www.alz.org/alzheimers-dementia/what-is-dementia/types-of-dementia/vascular-dementia

Alzheimer's Association. (n.d.-d). *What is dementia?* ALZ. https://www.alz.org/alzheimers-dementia/what-is-dementia

Alzheimer's Society. (2021, September 30). *Sundowning and dementia*. https://www.alzheimers.org.uk/about-dementia/symptoms-and-diagnosis/symptoms/sundowning

Alzheimer''s Society. (2022, February 23). *Jelly drops ""water sweets"" help to boost daily water intake*. https://www.alzheimers.org.uk/blog/jelly-drops-sweets-tackle-dehydration-dementia

Alzheimer's Society. (n.d.). *The dementia statements and rights-based approaches*. https://www.alzheimers.org.uk/dementia-professionals/dementia-experience-toolkit/dementia-statements-and-rights-based-approaches#:.

Anthem Memory Care. (2018, January 31). *Coping with dementia and sensory challenges: smell and taste*. https://www.anthemmemorycare.com/blog/coping-with-dementia-and-sensory-challenges-smell-and-taste#:.

Applewood Our House. (n.d.). *How virtual reality is making a difference in dementia care*. http://applewoodourhouse.com/how-virtual-reality-is-making-a-difference-in-dementia-care/#:.

Better Health Channel. (n.d.). *Dementia - early signs*. Better Health Channel

Department of Health & Human Services. https://www.betterhealth.vic.gov.au/health/conditionsandtreatments/dementia-early-signs

Bhardwaj, S., Kesari, K. K., Rachamalla, M., Mani, S., Ashraf, G. M., Jha, S. K., Kumar, P., Ambasta, R. K., Dureja, H., Devkota, H. P., Gupta, G., Chellappan, D. K., Singh, S. K., Dua, K., Ruokolainen, J., Kamal, M. A., Ojha, S., & Jha, N. K. (2022). CRISPR/Cas9 gene editing: New hope for Alzheimer''s disease therapeutics. *Journal of Advanced Research, 40,* 207–221. https://doi.org/10.1016/j.jare.2021.07.001

Cammisuli, D. M., Cipriani, G., Giusti, E. M., & Castelnuovo, G. (2022). Effects of reminiscence therapy on cognition, depression and quality of life in elderly people with Alzheimer''s Disease: A Systematic review of randomized Controlled trials. *Journal of Clinical Medicine, 11*(19), 5752. https://doi.org/10.3390/jcm11195752

Cherry, K. (2023, November 13). *What is the negativity bias?* Verywell Mind. https://www.verywellmind.com/negative-bias-4589618

Clear, J. (n.d.). Habit Stacking: How to build new habits by taking advantage of old ones. James Clear. https://jamesclear.com/habit-stacking

Cleveland Clinic. (n.d.). *Eat these foods to reduce stress and anxiety.* https://health.clevelandclinic.org/eat-these-foods-to-reduce-stress-and-anxiety

Concordia University. (n.d.). *Examples of cognitive restructuring.* https://www.concordia.ca/cunews/offices/provost/health/topics/stress-management/cognitive-restructuring--examples.html#:.

Cuncic, A., MA. (2023, January 23). *How to practice progressive muscle relaxation.* Verywell Mind. https://www.verywellmind.com/how-do-i-practice-progressive-muscle-relaxation-3024400

Davis, D. M., & Hayes, J. A. (n.d.). *What are the benefits of mindfulness.* https://www.apa.org. https://www.apa.org/monitor/2012/07-08/ce-corner

Dementia UK. (2023, October). *Music and dementia.* https://www.dementiauk.org/information-and-support/living-with-dementia/music-and-dementia/

Brain and Life, & Derrow, P. (2020, December). *What is dementia-related psychosis?* Brain and Life. https://www.brainandlife.org/articles/what-is-dementia-related-psychosis

Devere, R. (2017, June). *Music and dementia: An Overview.* Practical Neurology. https://practicalneurology.com/articles/2017-june/music-and-dementia-an-overview#:

DISB. (n.d). Understanding your health insurance. In *Government of the District of Columbia* [Report]. https://disb.dc.gov/sites/default/files/dc/sites/disb/page_content/attachments/DISB_CostSharingFactSheet_9.28.16.pdf

Family Caregiver Alliance. (n.d.). *Caregiver health.* https://www.caregiver.org/resource/caregiver-health/

Ferguson, S. (2022, December 20). *How to practice STOP mindfulness*. Psych Central. https://psychcentral.com/health/4-quick-mindfulness-techniques

Ferguson, S. (2023, April 20). *What is occupational therapy for dementia?* Healthline. https://www.healthline.com/health/dementia/occupational-therapy-for-dementia

Findley, C. (2024, February 22). *What are Alzheimer''s plaques and tangles?* Bright Focus. https://www.brightfocus.org/news/amyloid-plaques-and-neurofibril lary-tangles

Greater Good in Action. (2024, August 13). *Mindful breathing*. https://ggia.berkeley. edu/practice/mindful_breathing

Gregory, S. (2023, July 19). *Three promising drugs for treating Alzheimer''s disease bring fresh hope*. Alzheimer''s Society. https://www.alzheimers.org.uk/blog/ three-promising-drugs-for-treating-alzheimers-disease-bring-fresh-hope

Headspace. (n.d.). *What is mindfulness?* https://www.headspace.com/mindfulness/ mindfulness-101

Healthdirect. (n.d.). *Grief before death – understanding anticipatory grief*. https:// www.healthdirect.gov.au/understanding-anticipatory-grief#:.

Healthline. (2023, June 23). *Frontal Lobe: What to know*. https://www.healthline. com/human-body-maps/frontal-lobe#:.

Hipp, D. (2024, March 14). *Tips on how to redirect a loved one with dementia*. https:// www.aplaceformom.com/caregiver-resources/articles/redirect-a-loved-one-with-dementia#

Hope Health. (2023, July 6). *What palliative care means for Alzheimer''s and dementia*. HopeHealth. https://www.hopehealthco.org/blog/what-palliative-care-means-for-alzheimers-and-dementia/

Johns Hopkins Medicine. (2021, November 23). *Specialists in aging: Do you need a geriatrician?*https://www.hopkinsmedicine.org/health/wellness-and-preven tion/specialists-in-aging-do-you-need-a-geriatrician

Johns Hopkins Medicine. (2024, May 15). *Frontotemporal dementia*. https://www. hopkinsmedicine.org/health/conditions-and-diseases/dementia/frontotempo ral-dementia

K2 Medical Research. (n.d.). *Aging makes us more vulnerable to financial scams: Here''s how to spot them*. https://k2med.com/blog/aging-makes-us-more-vulner able-to-financial-scams-heres-how-to-spot-them/

Kilroy, A. (2023, January 27). *Differences of beneficiary designations vs. wills*. Smartas-set. https://smartasset.com/estate-planning/beneficiary-vs-will

Kinder Caring. (2024, June 1). Role of palliative care teams in pain management. *Kinder Caring*. https://kindercaring.com.au/palliative-care/role-of-palliative-care-teams-in-pain-management/

Kohlbrenner, B. (2022, May 24). *Dementia-associated sensory challenges: Tips for effective communication.* MedBridge Blog. https://www.medbridge.com/blog/ 2022/05/dementia-associated-sensory-challenges-tips-for-effective-commu nication/

Langmaid, S. (2024, August 4). *What are anti-amyloid therapies for Alzheimer''s disease?* WebMD. https://www.webmd.com/alzheimers/anti-amyloid-thera pies-alzheimers

Laurence, B. K. (2024, June 14). *What is social security disability?* www.nolo.com. https://www.nolo.com/legal-encyclopedia/social-security-disability-benefits- 29686.html

Lesley University. (n.d.). *6 Ways that art therapy can help people with memory loss.* https://lesley.edu/article/6-ways-that-art-therapy-can-help-people-with- memory-loss#:.

Livewell. (2021, May 21). *Why do people with dementia start eating too much or too little.* Livewell Care. https://livewell.care/why-do-people-with-dementia- start-eating-too-much-or-too-little/

Lsw, B. K. M. (2022, May 24). *Dementia-associated sensory challenges: Tips for effective communication.* MedBridge Blog. https://www.medbridge.com/blog/2022/05/ dementia-associated-sensory-challenges-tips-for-effective-communication/#:

Marcinkowska, M., Śniecikowska, J., Fajkis, N., Paśko, P., Franczyk, W., & Kołaczkowski, M. (2020). Management of Dementia-Related Psychosis, Agita- tion and Aggression: A review of the pharmacology and clinical effects of potential drug candidates. *CNS Drugs, 34*(3), 243–268. https://doi.org/10.1007/ s40263-020-00707-7

Mayo Clinic. (2021, July 29). *Vascular dementia.* https://www.mayoclinic.org/ diseases-conditions/vascular-dementia/symptoms-causes/syc-20378793

MedlinePlus. (n.d.). *Do-not-resuscitate order.* Medlineplus. https://medlineplus.gov/ ency/patientinstructions/000473.htm

Mindful Leader. (n.d.). *What are the three components of mindfulness?* https://www. mindfulleader.org/what-are-the-three-components-of-mindfulness#:.

Nidirect. (n.d.). *Communicating with a person living with a dementia.* Nidirect. https://www.nidirect.gov.uk/articles/communicating-person-living-dementia

NIH. (2024, April 30). *Study suggests treatments that unleash immune cells in the brain could help combat Alzheimer''s.* National Institute on Aging. https://www.nia. nih.gov/news/study-suggests-treatments-unleash-immune-cells-brain- could-help-combat-alzheimers#:.

NIH. (n.d.). *Lewy body dementia.* National Institute of Neurological Disorders and Stroke. https://www.ninds.nih.gov/health-information/disorders/lewy-body- dementia

Ravichandran, H. (2023, October 13). *What is the grandparent scam? How to identify*

& avoid it. Identity Guard. https://www.identityguard.com/news/grandparent-scam#:.

Raypole, C. (2022, December 5). *How to do a body scan meditation (and why you should)*. Healthline. https://www.healthline.com/health/body-scan-medita tion

Sampaio, A., Marques-Aleixo, I., Seabra, A., Mota, J., & Carvalho, J. (2021). Physical exercise for individuals with dementia: potential benefits perceived by formal caregivers. *BMC Geriatrics, 21*(1). https://doi.org/10.1186/s12877-020-01938-5

Segura, J. (2024, February 15). *Massive utility scam campaign spreads via online ads*. Malwarebytes. https://www.malwarebytes.com/blog/threat-intelligence/ 2024/02/massive-utility-scam-campaign-spreads-via-online-ads?srsltid= AfmBOopNg5wpCzFe3nyZcZj8wl65zkcCXekCgruOy5LAyqrpT4ZP6LsB

Stellar Care. (n.d.). *Elderly parent acting like child: What can I do?* https://stellar caresd.com/elderly-parent-acting-like-child/

Stroke Association. (n.d.). *What is vascular dementia?* https://www.stroke.org.uk/ stroke/effects/vascular-dementia#:.

The National Council on Aging. (2023a, August 22). *The National Council on Aging*. https://www.ncoa.org/article/does-medicaid-cover-memory-care

The National Council on Aging. (2023b, September 27). *Does long-term care insur-ance cover memory care? A comprehensive guide*. https://www.ncoa.org/article/ does-long-term-care-insurance-cover-memory-care-a-comprehensive-guide

The Ness Care Group. (n.d.). *Neuroplasticity what is it? And how can we use it in dementia treatment?* Ness Care, Dementia Care, Respite & Therapy. https://ness caregroup.co.uk/neuroplasticity-what-is-it-and-how-can-we-use-it-in-dementia-treatment/

The University of Toledo. (n.d.). *Deep breathing and relaxation*. https://www. utoledo.edu/studentaffairs/counseling/anxietytoolbox/breathingandrelax ation.html

Turco, A. (2024, April 26). *Learning boundaries: Navigating burnout and prioritizing Self-Care at every age*. Center for Hope & Health. https://www.centerforhope andhealth.com/blog/learning-boundaries-navigating-burnout-and-prioritiz ing-self-care-at-every-age/#:.

University of Cambridge. (2024, July 12). *Artificial intelligence outperforms clinical tests at predicting*. https://www.cam.ac.uk/research/news/artificial-intelli gence-outperforms-clinical-tests-at-predicting-progress-of-alzheimers-disease#

VeteranAid. (2018, January 9). *Alzheimer''s and dementia care for veterans*. https:// www.veteranaid.org/alzheimers-demnetia.php#:.

Watson, S. (2024, April 18). *Endorphins: The brain''s natural pain reliever*. Harvard

Health. https://www.health.harvard.edu/mind-and-mood/endorphins-the-brains-natural-pain-reliever

Wayne, M., White, M., & Robinson, L. (2024, April 29). *What is respite care?* Helpguide. https://www.helpguide.org/articles/caregiving/respite-care.htm

WebMD. (2022, January 11). *Recognizing caregiver burnout.* https://www.webmd.com/healthy-aging/caregiver-recognizing-burnout

WebMD. (2023, September 20). *How does mental health affect physical health?* https://www.webmd.com/mental-health/how-does-mental-health-affect-physical-health

Williams, C. L., & Tappen, R. M. (2008). Exercise training for depressed older adults with Alzheimer''s disease. *Aging & Mental Health, 12*(1), 72–80. https://doi.org/10.1080/13607860701529932

Woffindin, L. (2023, December 20). *All about the importance of pet therapy in care settings.* CPD Online College. https://cpdonline.co.uk/knowledge-base/care/pet-therapy-in-care-settings/#:.

World Health Organization. (2023, March 15). *Dementia.* WHO. https://www.who.int/news-room/fact-sheets/detail/dementia

Young, J. (2024, January 21). *Self- settled and third-party special needs trusts.* Tucson Elder Law Attorney. https://elder-law.com/self-settled-and-third-party-special-needs-trusts/

About the Author

About The Author

Debra Lewis RN, BSN is a registered nurse with a bachelor's degree in nursing and the author of *Dementia Caregiving 101*. She has also penned a compilation of short stories entitled *RN Real Nurse Stories Told by a Registered Nurse*.

Debra has practiced in multiple fields of nursing and has extensive knowledge across many medical specialties. Having cared for two parents with dementia, she knows the biggest challenges involved in caregiving. She has cared for critically ill people in hospital settings and provided home care for patients. Her experiences have given her a full-spectrum view into the progression and manifestation of dementia, and she shares effective strategies she uses and personal discoveries she has made in her work.